CAMBRIDGE SCHOOL

Shakespeare

The Sonnets

Edited by Rex Gibson

Series Editor: Rex Gibson
Director, Shakespeare and Schools Project

CAMBRIDGE
UNIVERSITY PRESS

PUBLISHED BY THE PRESS SYNDICATE OF THE UNIVERSITY OF CAMBRIDGE
The Pitt Building, Trumpington Street, Cambridge, United Kingdom

CAMBRIDGE UNIVERSITY PRESS
The Edinburgh Building, Cambridge CB2 2RU, UK
40 West 20th Street, New York, NY 10011–4211, USA
477 Williamstown Road, Port Melbourne, VIC 3207, Australia
Ruiz de Alarcón 13, 28014 Madrid, Spain
Dock House, The Waterfront, Cape Town 8001, South Africa

http://www.cambridge.org

First published 1997
Sixth printing 2002

Printed in the United Kingdom at the University Press, Cambridge

Typeset in Ehrhardt 11/13pt

A catalogue record for this book is available from the British Library.

Library of Congress Cataloguing in Publication data applied for

Designed by Richard Morris, Stonesfield Design
Picture research by Callie Kendall

Cover: *Unknown Man against a background of flames* by Nicholas Hilliard (1547–1619), Victoria and
Albert Museum P.5–1917.

ISBN 0 521 55947 2 paperback

Thanks are due to the following for permission to reproduce photographs:
jacket, by courtesy of the Board of Trustees of the Victoria and Albert Museum; 15, by the
permission of the Trustees of the Will of the 8th Earl of Berkeley, deceased; 33, reproduced by
courtesy of the Trustees, The National Gallery, London; 51, 65, reproduced by the permission
of the Board of Trustees of the Victoria and Albert Museum; 67, Martin Charles; 77, Rita Bailey;
93, The Master and Fellows of Corpus Christi College, Cambridge; 101, 146b, 181b, courtesy of
the National Portrait Gallery, London; 141t, Museum of London; 141b, A. F. Kersting; 146t,
Private Collection, on loan to the National Portrait Gallery, London; 148, By Kind Permission
of the Trustees of the Newdegate Settlement; 151, by permission of the British Library,
London; 179t, The Royal Collection © Her Majesty Queen Elizabeth II; 179b, Arundel Castle,
Sussex/Bridgeman Art Library, London; 181t, Reproduced by permission of the Marquess of
Bath, Longleat House, Warminster, Wiltshire/photograph Courtauld Institute of Art.

Contents

Cambridge School Shakespeare

This edition of *The Sonnets* is part of the *Cambridge School Shakespeare* series. Like the plays in the series, it has been specially prepared to help all students in schools and colleges.

Three warning voices have influenced this edition. The first is that of the great eighteenth-century critic, Dr Samuel Johnson. For him, notes on a poem were 'necessary evils'. He urged anyone who wished to gain 'the highest pleasure' to read Shakespeare 'with utter negligence of all his commentators'.

The second caution is a single line by the poet William Wordsworth: 'we murder to dissect'. Treating poetry as if it were a body to be cut up can kill it. Over-analysis is the death of any poem.

The third voice is that of the poet John Keats, who saw Shakespeare as a man 'capable of being in uncertainties, mysteries, doubts, without any irritable reaching after fact and reason'. This same quality helps any reader of poetry. It recognises the importance of imaginative response, and does not seek to tie a poem down to a single meaning. It accepts that poetry delights in playing with language, and that different interpretations are possible and desirable.

These warning voices have influenced the way in which this edition aims to help you make up your own mind about *The Sonnets*, rather than having someone else's interpretation and judgement handed down to you. It will be of value to you whether you are studying for an examination or reading for pleasure, working alone or with a group of other students. You know your own needs and interests, and can use the help provided in ways appropriate to your own purposes.

Each sonnet is presented with accompanying material which aims to enrich your own experience of the poem. You will find help with unfamiliar words, with imagery, and with other 'poetic' features, as well as suggestions for practical work. There are also notes to increase your understanding of the language and themes of the sonnets, and of the historical and literary climate in which they were written.

But remember that the sonnet itself is always infinitely more valuable than any commentary.

Rex Gibson

This edition of *The Sonnets* uses the text established by G. Blakemore Evans in *The New Cambridge Shakespeare*.

What is a sonnet?

A sonnet is a fourteen-line poem written in iambic pentameter.

Definitions of poetry can be boring, dangerous and wrong. Boring, because they often get in the way of reading the poetry itself. Dangerous, because they may encourage over-analysis and so 'murder' any poem. Wrong, because poets, and Shakespeare in particular, never follow any rule slavishly and mechanically, and so do not fit any one definition neatly. Keep these warnings in mind as you read what follows, which is intended to help you to understand the structure and style of a sonnet.

A Shakespearean sonnet is made up of three quatrains and a couplet (sometimes written as 4 + 4 + 4 + 2). A quatrain is four lines of verse. The couplet is the final two lines of verse. The rhyme scheme is ABAB CDCD EFEF GG. So, the structure of Sonnet 73 could be set out as:

Quatrain 1 (lines 1–4)	Rhyme scheme
That time of year thou mayst in me behold	A
When yellow leaves, or none, or few, do hang	B
Upon those boughs which shake against the cold,	A
Bare ruined choirs, where late the sweet birds sang.	B

Quatrain 2 (lines 5–8)	
In me thou seest the twilight of such day	C
As after sunset fadeth in the west,	D
Which by and by black night doth take away,	C
Death's second self, that seals up all in rest.	D

Quatrain 3 (lines 9–12)	
In me thou seest the glowing of such fire	E
That on the ashes of his youth doth lie,	F
As the death-bed whereon it must expire,	E
Consumed with that which it was nourished by.	F

Couplet (lines 13–14)	
This thou perceiv'st, which makes thy love more strong,	G
To love that well which thou must leave ere long.	G

You may find it helpful to think of a sonnet as a little story or scene. It explores and resolves a thought or an experience, and frequently contains a urn', or change of thought. Lines 1–12 often develop an argument or give accumulating examples. The couplet (lines 13–14) draws a conclusion (sometimes witty), or acts as a sting in the tail, ironically pointing up a paradox, or contradicting the preceding twelve lines. In Sonnet 73, each quatrain contains different images of old age: trees in winter and ruined churches (quatrain 1); sunset and a dying fire (quatrains 2 and 3). The couplet is a sharp reminder that the signs of old age and approaching death make the need for love even more acute.

Shakespeare's sonnets are written in iambic pentameter (a technical description of how the rhythm is measured). Each line has five stresses in the rhythm. Pentameter comes from the Greek 'penta' meaning five, and 'meter' meaning measure. Typically, the five stressed (/) syllables alternate with five unstressed (x) syllables, giving a ten-syllable line. When you begin to study poetry, it can be helpful to tap out the stresses:

> x / x / x / x / x /
> That time of year thou mayst in me behold

You can already see the dangers which can arise when poetry is analysed in this way. It begins to look like algebra, and seems to suggest a mechanical, repetitive rhythm:

> de dum, de dum, de dum, de dum, de dum.

However, the rhythm of Shakespeare's sonnets is infinitely flexible and varied. It is vital to remember that the 'weight' of each stress can vary, and that the spaces, or pauses, in a line can be of different lengths.

Iambic pentameter is not like the beat in synthesised electronic music, where the rhythm is unvaried and unvarying. Just as the human heartbeat is not exactly regular, but has tiny unnoticed variations, so iambic pentameter is a human, rather than a mechanical measure. Poetry which is exactly regular becomes doggerel. Shakespeare's skill ensures that each line has the potential for rhythmical variation, and he sometimes writes lines of more than ten syllables (for example, Sonnets 20 and 87).

Remember, Shakespeare does not slavishly follow any formula. His sequence includes sonnets of fifteen and twelve lines (Sonnets 99 and 126). He varies the sonnet structure, for example as 12 + 2 (Sonnet 66). Other sonnets can be read as 8 + 6 or 8 + 4 + 2. The 'turn' of the sonnet can come before the couplet, usually at line 9. Within the seemingly restricting limit of fourteen lines, Shakespeare experiments restlessly and continuously, and achieves great variety.

Introducing *The Sonnets*

Only three facts are certain about Shakespeare's sonnets: they were first mentioned in 1598 by Francis Meres, a Cambridge schoolmaster and cleric, who wrote of Shakespeare's 'sugared sonnets among his private friends'; two sonnets were published in 1599; the full sequence of 154 sonnets was first published in 1609.

Beyond these few facts, nothing else is known for certain. For example, no one really knows if Shakespeare himself authorised publication of the sonnets – someone may have done it without his permission. Neither is it known if they appear in the order which Shakespeare intended. For over three centuries, many people have rearranged the sequence in ways which they argue are more convincing. There is just as much disagreement about exactly when the sonnets were written. Although many sonnets echo the style of Shakespeare's earlier plays, claims have been made for all dates, ranging from 1585 to 1609.

The fiercest arguments rage over whether the sonnets are autobiographical, or whether they are literary exercises. Some people claim that the sonnets are purely fictitious, saying that Shakespeare was exercising his imagination and poetic skills on themes that many other poets had written about (see pages 178–81).

Others hold a totally different point of view, claiming that the sonnets are, in effect, Shakespeare's personal diary, recording actual events in his life, and reflecting his true thoughts and feelings. They argue that the sonnets tell a story which, in outline, looks like this:

Sonnets 1–126 are written to a young man. Sonnets 127–54 concern a woman who has come to be known as 'the dark lady'. Shakespeare becomes increasingly friendly with the young man, who is of high social status. At first, he simply urges the young man to marry and have children. But Shakespeare's feelings become so strong that he desires to immortalise his friend in verse, and is tortured by any separation, and by the thought that his friend cares more for a rival poet. The dark lady causes Shakespeare more emotional pain. She is his mistress, but is unfaithful to him both with the young man and with other men. The sonnets criticise her looks and her morals. Shakespeare expresses self-disgust at his feelings for her.

Pages 93, 101 and 146–8 present speculations about the identity of the young man, the dark lady, and the rival poet.

Among those who claim that *The Sonnets* are Shakespeare's most personal writing was the poet William Wordsworth. He argued that the sonnets revealed Shakespeare's intimate thoughts, 'with this key Shakespeare unlocked his heart'. On the other hand, the critic Robert Browning fiercely rejected Wordsworth's claim, contemptuously retorting, 'Did Shakespeare? If so, the less Shakespeare he!'. Browning was challenging the view that it is possible to deduce from poems or plays the beliefs or life story of the poet or playwright.

The differing views of Wordsworth and Browning have been echoed in the judgements of a host of critics:

'inspired by real love and friendship'	'… only following tradition, and exercising his imagination'
'remarkable confessions of his youthful errors'	'merely effusions of his poetic fancy'
'authentic records of Shakespeare's life'	'… give no access to his personal history'

Whether *The Sonnets* are autobiographical or just literary exercises, they read like the thoughts of someone on the rack, tortured by conflicting emotions, their nerve ends exposed as they painfully explore their most intimate feelings. That is why, throughout this edition, the commentary on many of the sonnets uses Shakespeare's name. *The Sonnets* may arise partly from intensely felt personal experience, but it is impossible to link them precisely to actual events in Shakespeare's life.

A similarly wide range of views has been expressed as to why Shakespeare wrote *The Sonnets*. Was it to clarify his feelings? To test his poetic skills? For the amusement of a small circle of friends? For the eyes of just one or two individuals? To take part in the fashion of the time for writing sonnets? No one knows for sure.

In order to make up your own mind about the extent to which you think *The Sonnets* reveal Shakespeare's life and feelings, it may be helpful to think of his plays. Macbeth kills a king, Othello strangles his wife. But Shakespeare did neither of these things. The words and actions of Macbeth and Othello, and of every other character in the plays, cannot be taken as reflecting Shakespeare's own life and beliefs.

However, the most important questions concern the poetic quality of the sonnets themselves. Such questions are addressed throughout this edition.

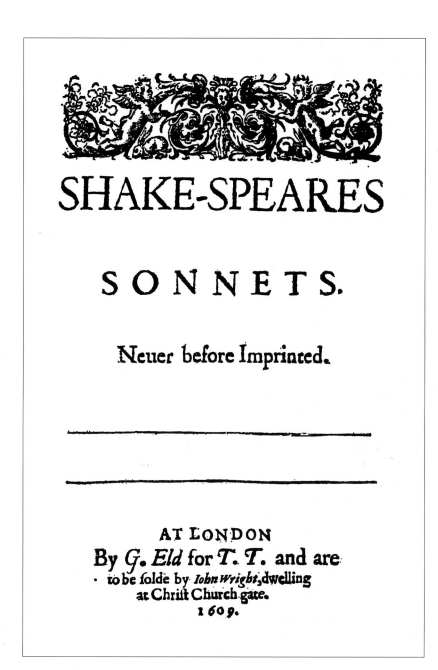

The title page of the first edition of Shakespeare's *Sonnets*,
published in 1609. Only thirteen copies of the original edition survive today.

TO.THE.ONLIE.BEGETTER.OF.
THESE.INSVING.SONNETS.
Mr.W.H. ALL.HAPPINESSE.
AND.THAT.ETERNITIE.
PROMISED.
BY.
OVR.EVER–LIVING.POET.
WISHETH.
THE.WELL-WISHING.
ADVENTVRER.IN.
SETTING.
FORTH.

T. T.

The dedication above appears in the first edition of *The Sonnets*, published in 1609. T.T. is Thomas Thorpe, the publisher. It seems to have been his custom to write dedications in this lapidary style (as if engraved on stone).

One interpretation is that Thomas Thorpe dedicates *The Sonnets* to the person who inspired them, 'the onlie begetter'. He is Mr W.H., the young man who has been promised immortalisation in verse by Shakespeare ('our ever-living poet').

Who was Mr W.H.? Many suggestions have been made, but his identity is still unproven. The two main candidates are Henry Wriothesley (pronounced 'Risley'), Earl of Southampton, and William Herbert, Earl of Pembroke. You can find out more about them on page 146.

In the last five lines, Thorpe compares himself to an adventurer or explorer setting out on a sea voyage. Just as such brave travellers set forth to explore the world, so *The Sonnets* are set in print and are also embarking on their journey.

A quite different interpretation of the dedication argues that 'the onlie begetter' does not refer to the person who inspired *The Sonnets*, but to the person who procured Shakespeare's manuscript for the publisher. Possible candidates include: William Hathaway (Shakespeare's brother-in-law), William Hall (a printer), Sir William Harvey (stepfather of the Earl of Southampton), and even 'William Himself' (Shakespeare).

I

From fairest creatures we desire increase,
That thereby beauty's rose might never die,
But as the riper should by time decease,
His tender heir might bear his memory: 4
But thou, contracted to thine own bright eyes,
Feed'st thy light's flame with self-substantial fuel,
Making a famine where abundance lies,
Thyself thy foe, to thy sweet self too cruel.   8
Thou that art now the world's fresh ornament,
And only herald to the gaudy spring,
Within thine own bud buriest thy content,
And, tender churl, mak'st waste in niggarding: 12
    Pity the world, or else this glutton be,
    To eat the world's due, by the grave and thee.

Sonnet 1 introduces the theme of the first seventeen sonnets, namely an attempt to persuade the young man to marry and have children, ensuring that his beauty will outlast his own death. The sonnet claims that all beautiful living things ('fairest creatures') should have offspring ('increase') in order to carry on their loveliness. But the young man, in love with himself, refuses to have children. Like a miser, he wastefully hoards his beauty.

The sonnet employs the imagery of flowers ('rose', 'bud'), a traditional feature of love poetry. Another powerful image is that of food, suggesting that everything in life needs nourishment. By feeding only his self-admiration and by dying childless, the young man denies the world its right ('due'): his beautiful children.

As you read Sonnets 1–17, notice the way in which Shakespeare uses many different images to try to persuade his friend to marry and have children.

---

the riper the older
tender heir young loving child
contracted to betrothed to, loving only
Feed'st ... fuel admire only yourself

fresh ornament newest decoration
gaudy joyous
content children, happiness
tender churl young skinflint, miser
niggarding hoarding your beauty

2

When forty winters shall besiege thy brow,
And dig deep trenches in thy beauty's field,
Thy youth's proud livery so gazed on now
Will be a tottered weed of small worth held: 4
Then being asked, where all thy beauty lies,
Where all the treasure of thy lusty days,
To say within thine own deep-sunken eyes
Were an all-eating shame, and thriftless praise.   8
How much more praise deserved thy beauty's use,
If thou could'st answer, 'This fair child of mine
Shall sum my count, and make my old excuse',
Proving his beauty by succession thine.   12
    This were to be new made when thou art old,
    And see thy blood warm when thou feel'st it cold.

Sonnet 2 attempts to persuade the young man that, by fathering a child, he can ensure that his beauty continues, even though his own looks will fade with age. Military imagery conveys the way in which time destroys the beauty of youth ('besiege', 'trenches', 'field', 'livery'). Throughout the sonnet, legal and financial language develops the notion of beauty as wealth: 'worth', 'treasure', 'thriftless', 'use' (investment, usury), 'sum my count' (be the total of my life's account), 'Proving' (administering a will) and 'succession' (inheritance).

    Like all of Sonnets 1–17, this sonnet is structured as a logical argument intended to persuade the young man to marry and have children. As you read it, think about how it could be spoken to increase its persuasive power. For example, decide which words or phrases you would emphasise to convince the young man that, when he is old and no longer admired, his child's inherited beauty will keep him young.

deep trenches wrinkles	**tottered weed** ragged garment
field face (battlefield)	**lusty days** vigorous youth
proud livery beautiful face	**thriftless** profitless
(splendid uniform)	**make my old excuse** justify my age

3

Look in thy glass and tell the face thou viewest,
Now is the time that face should form another,
Whose fresh repair if now thou not renewest,
Thou dost beguile the world, unbless some mother.   4
For where is she so fair whose uneared womb
Disdains the tillage of thy husbandry?
Or who is he so fond will be the tomb
Of his self-love to stop posterity?   8
Thou art thy mother's glass, and she in thee
Calls back the lovely April of her prime;
So thou through windows of thine age shalt see,
Despite of wrinkles, this thy golden time.   12
   But if thou live rememb'red not to be,
   Die single, and thine image dies with thee.

The young man is reminded that, just as he perpetuates his mother's youthful loveliness, so any children he has will continue his own beauty. The image of a mirror ('glass') runs through the sonnet: the young man's own reflected beauty (lines 1 and 14), the young man mirroring his mother's beauty (line 9), the young man's child reflecting his beauty (lines 11–12).

The fruitfulness of good farming ('husbandry') is used as a sexual metaphor, to claim that many women would willingly be the mother of the young man's child. 'Uneared' and 'tillage' both imply ploughing, which, like sexual intercourse, brings forth new life.

Line 10, 'Calls back the lovely April of her prime', recalls springtime in England when the countryside, blossoming into life, has great beauty. As *The Sonnets* are read all over the world, suggest an equivalent metaphor for a country in which April produces a completely different season.

---

beguile cheat
unbless deprive (of a child)
uneared unploughed, not yet fruitful
Disdains the tillage scorns the
  ploughing (would not have sexual
  intercourse)

fond foolish, loving
posterity descendants
windows spectacles
rememb'red commemorated

4

Unthrifty loveliness, why dost thou spend
Upon thyself thy beauty's legacy?
Nature's bequest gives nothing, but doth lend,
And being frank she lends to those are free: 4
Then, beauteous niggard, why dost thou abuse
The bounteous largess given thee to give?
Profitless usurer, why dost thou use
So great a sum of sums, yet canst not live? 8
For having traffic with thyself alone,
Thou of thyself thy sweet self dost deceive:
Then how when Nature calls thee to be gone,
What àcceptable audit canst thou leave? 12
    Thy unused beauty must be tombed with thee,
    Which usèd lives th'executor to be.

The dominant imagery of Sonnet 4 is of finance and investment. There is a sustained contrast throughout between the young man's miserliness in refusing to have children, and the generosity of Nature, which lends its gifts freely. With the exception of lines 10 and 11, every line contains at least one word which has echoes of commerce or wealth (for example, 'Unthrifty' and 'spend' in line 1).

The argument of the sonnet is conducted through question and answer. The four questions have an insistent accusatory tone ('why', 'why', 'why', 'What'). They address the young man in uncomplimentary terms: 'Unthrifty' (wasteful), 'niggard' (miser) and 'usurer' (harsh money-lender).

Try reading the sonnet in an accusing tone of voice. Make line 14 an emphatic statement of how such waste of beauty should be avoided. Do you think such a tone is appropriate?

legacy inheritance
Nature's bequest... lend Nature only loans her gifts
frank generous, bountiful
free generous
largess gifts

live have children
traffic commerce, trade
audit account of your life
unused not invested
executor administrator of a will

5

Those hours that with gentle work did frame
The lovely gaze where every eye doth dwell
Will play the tyrants to the very same,
And that unfair which fairly doth excel;   4
For never-resting time leads summer on
To hideous winter and confounds him there,
Sap checked with frost and lusty leaves quite gone,
Beauty o'ersnowed and bareness every where: 8
Then were not summer's distillation left
A liquid prisoner pent in walls of glass,
Beauty's effect with beauty were bereft,
Nor it nor no remembrance what it was.   12
    But flowers distilled, though they with winter meet,
    Leese but their show; their substance still lives sweet.

Sonnet 5 reminds the young man of the destructive effects of time. Although Time creates beauty, it will surely destroy it, just as the ravages of winter follow the abundance of summer. The final six lines argue that the essence of summer can live on in perfume made from flowers. Although perfume is made by destroying flowers' appearance, it ensures that their essential beauty and the memory of that beauty survive. The metaphor of perfume will be used in the next sonnet to persuade the young man to have a child to ensure his beauty survives his death.

Sonnet 5 contains examples of language use which recur throughout *The Sonnets*. Look out for further examples as you read on, such as:

personification turning time into a person ('never-resting time').

vivid description the closely observed accuracy of lines 7 and 8.

word-play creating new words (the adjective 'fair' is turned into a verb, 'un-fair'); using the same word to different effect ('unfair'/'fairly').

The lovely gaze (the young man)
play the tyrants behave cruelly
unfair make ugly
confounds destroys

summer's distillation the essence of summer (perfume distilled from flowers)
pent trapped
bereft stripped, despoiled
Leese lose

6

Then let not winter's ragged hand deface
In thee thy summer ere thou be distilled:
Make sweet some vial; treasure thou some place
With beauty's treasure ere it be self-killed: 4
That use is not forbidden usury
Which happies those that pay the willing loan;
That's for thyself to breed another thee,
Or ten times happier be it ten for one;   8
Ten times thyself were happier than thou art,
If ten of thine ten times refigured thee:
Then what could death do if thou shouldst depart,
Leaving thee living in posterity?   12
    Be not self-willed, for thou art much too fair
    To be death's conquest and make worms thine heir.

Sonnet 6 continues the thought expressed in Sonnet 5. It begins with 'Then', and the summer/winter theme recurs. The image of beauty distilled into perfume now develops into a plea to make some woman pregnant ('make sweet some vial') so that a child will continue the young man's beauty.

Repetition in poetry can enrich meaning and emotional appeal. A repeated word, or variations of a word, invites the reader to respond to its different possible meanings. Here, such repeated words are 'treasure' (lines 3 and 4), 'use'/'usury' (line 5), 'happies'/'happier' (lines 6, 8 and 9). The five-fold repetition of 'Ten' is a reminder that, in Shakespeare's time, the maximum rate of interest was fixed by law at ten per cent. It echoes the money-lending image in Sonnet 4.

Read Sonnets 5 and 6 as a single poem of twenty-eight lines to experience how they are linked. Do you think that Sonnets 4, 5 and 6 could also make a single poem?

---

ere before
vial womb (the image is of the glass perfume-bottle in Sonnet 5)
usury lending money at high interest

breed create (like interest on an investment)
refigured reproduced
posterity future time
conquest property, booty

7

Lo in the orient when the gracious light
Lifts up his burning head, each under eye
Doth homage to his new-appearing sight,
Serving with looks his sacred majesty;   4
And having climbed the steep-up heavenly hill,
Resembling strong youth in his middle age,
Yet mortal looks adore his beauty still,
Attending on his golden pilgrimage: 8
But when from highmost pitch, with weary car,
Like feeble age he reeleth from the day,
The eyes (fore duteous) now converted are
From his low tract and look another way: 12
    So thou, thyself outgoing in thy noon,
    Unlooked on diest, unless thou get a son.

The intention of Sonnet 7 is to encourage the young man to marry and have children. Consider how each of the following adds to the poem's persuasive appeal:

Echoes of nature The young man's beauty is compared to the sun's daily journey. Its majesty is worshipped and admired at sunrise and noon (youth and maturity), but is ignored at sunset (old age).

Echoes of classical mythology The sun was regarded as a chariot ('car') driven across the sky by Phaethon (the son of the Greek sun-god, Helios).

Echoes of religion 'Religious' words recur throughout: 'Lo', 'gracious', 'homage', 'sacred', 'heavenly', 'pilgrimage', 'converted', 'tract'. Line 1 even reads like the opening of a hymn.

Echoes of 'sun'/'son' Although the word 'sun' does not appear in the sonnet, the sun is the dominant image. There is implicit linking of 'sun' with 'son' throughout.

---

orient East
light sun
under eye watcher on earth, subject
homage worship, reverence
highmost pitch zenith (highest point)

weary car sunset (like an exhausted chariot-driver)
fore duteous previously dutiful
tract path

8

Music to hear, why hear'st thou music sadly?
Sweets with sweets war not, joy delights in joy:
Why lov'st thou that which thou receiv'st not gladly,
Or else receiv'st with pleasure thine annoy?   4
If the true concord of well-tunèd sounds,
By unions married, do offend thine ear,
They do but sweetly chide thee, who confounds
In singleness the parts that thou shouldst bear;   8
Mark how one string, sweet husband to another,
Strikes each in each by mutual ordering;
Resembling sire, and child, and happy mother,
Who all in one, one pleasing note do sing;   12
    Whose speechless song being many, seeming one,
    Sings this to thee, 'Thou single wilt prove none.'

The metaphor of music is used in order to urge the young man to marry
and have children. Just as the sounds from a single lute string combine
with sounds from other strings to produce harmony, so father, mother
and child are an ideal and harmonious combination. Such harmony re-
proaches the young man for his 'single' (unmarried) state.

The first quatrain raises a question which still perplexes people today:
why do we seem to gain pleasure from things we find painful or sadden-
ing? The sonnet uses the analogy of music, and lines 1–2 are a reminder
of Jessica in *The Merchant of Venice*, who says, 'I am never merry when I
hear sweet music'.

Another analogy could be the feeling many people experience when
watching a tragedy in the theatre. Terrible things happen in *King Lear*,
evoking all kinds of painful emotions. Yet audiences return again and
again, clearly 'enjoying' the play. Suggest your own answer to the question posed in lines 3–4.

---

thine annoy what pains you
concord agreement, harmony
unions married harmony, marriage
chide rebuke
confounds destroys, ruins

parts roles, talents, melodies, sexual
  organs
bear play, sing, support, use
sire father

A miniature by Nicholas Hilliard of Queen Elizabeth I playing a lute. In Shakespeare's time, music was often used as a metaphor for order and harmony in society and nature. Musical concord implied agreement and co-operation, and was claimed to mirror the 'natural harmony' of the family, of society at large, and of the cosmos itself. Shakespeare frequently used this (now fiercely disputed) key idea of Renaissance thought. See, for example, *Troilus and Cressida*, Act 1 Scene 3, lines 78–124.

9

Is it for fear to wet a widow's eye
That thou consum'st thyself in single life?
Ah! if thou issueless shalt hap to die,
The world will wail thee like a makeless wife;   4
The world will be thy widow and still weep,
That thou no form of thee hast left behind,
When every private widow well may keep,
By children's eyes, her husband's shape in mind: 8
Look what an unthrift in the world doth spend
Shifts but his place, for still the world enjoys it,
But beauty's waste hath in the world an end,
And kept unused the user so destroys it: 12
    No love toward others in that bosom sits
    That on himself such murd'rous shame commits.

The grief a widow feels for her dead husband is compared with the grief the world would feel if the young man were to die without leaving a child to carry on his beauty. A widow has children to remind her of her dead husband (lines 7–8). Similarly, money may be wasted, but it still remains in circulation (lines 9–10). In contrast, beauty dies once and for all (lines 11–12). Therefore, remaining unmarried and childless is a crime which reflects a lack of love for others.

Alliteration (the repetition of the first letter of a word) helps to enrich poetic effect. Throughout the sonnet, 'w' is repeated, beginning with 'wet a widow's eye' in line 1. Imagine that one of Shakespeare's friends said to him, on reading the sonnet, 'Wouldn't "mourn" be better than "wail" in line 4? And do the five repetitions of "world" really strengthen the sonnet or weaken it?' Make Shakespeare's reply.

---

consum'st eat (see Sonnet 1, line 14)
issueless childless
hap happen
makeless mateless (without a husband)
still always

unthrift wastrel, prodigal (see Sonnets 2, 4 and 6)
Shifts but his place merely goes into someone else's pocket
murd'rous shame shameful murder

For shame deny that thou bear'st love to any,
Who for thyself art so unprovident.
Grant, if thou wilt, thou art beloved of many,
But that thou none lov'st is most evident;   4
For thou art so possessed with murd'rous hate,
That 'gainst thyself thou stick'st not to conspire,
Seeking that beauteous roof to ruinate
Which to repair should be thy chief desire: 8
O change thy thought, that I may change my mind!
Shall hate be fairer lodged than gentle love?
Be as thy presence is, gracious and kind,
Or to thyself at least kind-hearted prove: 12
    Make thee another self for love of me,
    That beauty still may live in thine or thee.

Lines 1–8 appear to be sharply critical in tone. They accuse the young man of loving no one, being full of self-destructive hate. But lines 9–14 are a plea: that the young man change inwardly to match his beautiful outward appearance ('presence'), and that he father a child to ensure his beauty lives on.

The 'roof' which needs to be repaired (line 7) may signify either 'body', or 'house' in the sense of a noble family or great country house. The sonnet may, therefore, be a plea to an aristocratic young man to repair his family's fortunes. (The young man of the sonnets was apparently of much higher social status than Shakespeare. See page 146.)

However, line 13, 'for love of me' (for my sake), suggests that there is a very close or equal friendship between Shakespeare and the young man. Do you think that the sonnet has an intimate, personal tone, or does it sound more like someone speaking to his social superior?

---

bear'st feel
unprovident reckless, wasteful
possessed wickedly filled
stick'st not don't hesitate
repair maintain
be fairer lodged live in a more
  beautiful place

kind-hearted loving to your kin
  (kind)
still always
thine or thee your children or
  yourself

11

As fast as thou shalt wane, so fast thou grow'st
In one of thine, from that which thou departest,
And that fresh blood which youngly thou bestow'st
Thou mayst call thine, when thou from youth convertest: 4
Herein lives wisdom, beauty, and increase,
Without this, folly, age, and cold decay:
If all were minded so, the times should cease,
And threescore year would make the world away.   8
Let those whom Nature hath not made for store,
Harsh, featureless, and rude, barrenly perish:
Look whom she best endowed she gave the more;
Which bounteous gift thou shouldst in bounty cherish: 12
    She carved thee for her seal, and meant thereby,
    Thou shouldst print more, not let that copy die.

The sonnet claims that children guarantee the continuance of humanity's good qualities. It reminds the young man that, if everyone behaved like him and refused to have children, all life would cease. Nature intends people endowed with superior qualities to have children. This idea raises uncomfortable questions today:

a Do lines 9–11 anticipate Darwin's theory of 'survival of the fittest'? Think about whether or not they could be interpreted in that way.

b Are lines 9–11 socially dangerous? The surface meaning seems to be that ugly ('featureless') people are not intended to survive. Only the 'best endowed' (with excellent qualities) deserve to have children. Is this the ideology of 'the master race'?

The questions in a and b raise the issue of the relationship between poetry and politics. Do you think questions of politics are irrelevant to the study and enjoyment of Shakespeare's sonnets? Give reasons for your reply.

---

wane grow old
departest leave behind
bestow'st gave
convertest change
increase life
make the world away end all
  human life on earth

store breeding
barrenly perish die childless
in bounty cherish multiply lovingly
seal stamp (for making impressions
  in wax)

12

When I do count the clock that tells the time,
And see the brave day sunk in hideous night,
When I behold the violet past prime,
And sable curls all silvered o'er with white,   4
When lofty trees I see barren of leaves,
Which erst from heat did canopy the herd,
And summer's green all girded up in sheaves
Borne on the bier with white and bristly beard: 8
Then of thy beauty do I question make
That thou among the wastes of time must go,
Since sweets and beauties do themselves forsake,
And die as fast as they see others grow,   12
    And nothing 'gainst Time's scythe can make defence
    Save breed to brave him when he takes thee hence.

Sonnet 12 broods on the remorseless effect of Time, as it destroys all beauty. Only by having children can humanity defy the finality of death. Suggest how each of the following adds to the sonnet's power:

a The sonnet is one long sentence. This intensifies the cumulative effect of Time, as the sustained imagery lists all the things which it destroys (for example, day, violet, curls, trees).

b The many antitheses (contrasts) increase the feeling of Time's ruinous power: 'brave day'/'hideous night', 'sable'/'white', and so on.

c The first words of each line (for instance, 'When', 'And', 'When') create an accumulating and urgent sense of the fatal power of Time.

d The frequent alliteration throughout the sonnet (which, in line 1, combines with monosyllables to resemble the ticking of a clock).

e The image in line 13 of Time as a deadly harvester, cutting down humanity with a scythe.

f The final line strikes a note of defiance against Time's ravages.

---

past prime beyond its best
sable black
erst previously
canopy shelter
girded bound, tied

bier farm wagon (or platform for corpses)
themselves forsake depart from themselves
breed offspring, children
brave (line 14) defy

13

O that you were your self! but, love, you are
No longer yours than you yourself here live;
Against this coming end you should prepare,
And your sweet semblance to some other give: 4
So should that beauty which you hold in lease
Find no determination; then you were
Your self again after yourself's decease,
When your sweet issue your sweet form should bear.   8
Who lets so fair a house fall to decay,
Which husbandry in honour might uphold
Against the stormy gusts of winter's day
And barren rage of death's eternal cold?   12
   O none but unthrifts: dear my love, you know
   You had a father, let your son say so.

The young man is reminded that he will not live for ever, his beauty is only loaned ('in lease') to him. Fathering a child is the only way of ensuring that beauty survives after death. Sonnet 13 contains less imagery than Sonnet 12, but it echoes the imagery of property and finance which appeared in earlier sonnets: 'lease', 'determination' (ending of a lease), 'husbandry'.

There seems to be evidence of a closer relationship between the poet and the young man, who is called 'love' in line 1 and 'dear my love' in line 13. Up to this point in the sonnet sequence, Shakespeare has used 'thou' or 'thy' in addressing the young man.

Now, Shakespeare uses 'you', a much more intimate form of address in Elizabethan times. The sonnet includes seventeen uses of 'you', 'yours' or 'yourself'. Emphasise them to yourself as you read, and see if you think they suggest a feeling of a close relationship.

Against in expectation of
semblance appearance
in lease on loan
determination end
issue children

house body, family, kin (see Sonnet
  10, lines 7–8)
husbandry good housekeeping,
  marriage
unthrifts wasters, prodigals

Not from the stars do I my judgement pluck,
And yet methinks I have astronomy,
But not to tell of good or evil luck,
Of plagues, of dearths, or seasons' quality;   4
Nor can I fortune to brief minutes tell,
Pointing to each his thunder, rain, and wind,
Or say with princes if it shall go well
By oft predict that I in heaven find: 8
But from thine eyes my knowledge I derive,
And, constant stars, in them I read such art
As truth and beauty shall together thrive
If from thy self to store thou wouldst convert: 12
     Or else of thee this I prognosticate,
     Thy end is truth's and beauty's doom and date.

The image which runs through this sonnet is of astrology, or predicting the future by observation of the stars. Shakespeare uses the image to claim that he can predict only one thing, namely that truth and beauty will live on only if the young man has a child. If he does not, truth and beauty will die when he dies.

You may find it helpful to identify in lines 3–8 all the things that astrologers traditionally predicted. In line 7, 'it' could mean 'the future', but don't be afraid to suggest possibilities of your own.

One definition of poetry is 'the best words in the best order'. Imagine that Shakespeare's first drafts of lines 4 and 6 were as follows:

line 4 'Of dearths and plagues, and seasons' quality'
line 6 'Fixing in each his rain, thunder and wind'.

Suggest what thoughts Shakespeare may have had as he rewrote the two lines in order to achieve the final version.

---

my judgement pluck gain my knowledge
have astronomy understand astrology
dearths famines
fortune ... tell make precise predictions to the very minute
oft predict frequent predictions
constant never-changing
store breeding children
convert change
prognosticate predict
doom and date doomsday, death

When I consider every thing that grows
Holds in perfection but a little moment,
That this huge stage presenteth nought but shows
Whereon the stars in secret influence comment;   4
When I perceive that men as plants increase,
Cheerèd and checked even by the selfsame sky,
Vaunt in their youthful sap, at height decrease,
And wear their brave state out of memory: 8
Then the conceit of this inconstant stay
Sets you most rich in youth before my sight,
Where wasteful Time debateth with Decay
To change your day of youth to sullied night,   12
    And all in war with Time for love of you,
    As he takes from you, I ingraft you new.

The theme of Sonnet 15 is the transience of human life. Youth only flourishes briefly before Time brings inevitable decay and death. But the concluding couplet makes a claim which will recur in later sonnets, saying that, after his death, the young man will live on in Shakespeare's poetry. *The Sonnets* will ensure his immortality.

An image of natural growth runs through the sonnet ('grows', 'plants', 'sap', 'ingraft'). Lines 3 and 4 contain a theatrical image: 'stage' (world), 'shows' (brief appearances by actors). Like an Elizabethan audience, 'the stars' comment on the actors.

The opening words ('When I consider …') establish a reflective tone which continues into the second and third quatrains. These quatrains begin with 'When' and 'Then', showing how the thought ('conceit') of the brevity of beauty leads the poet to think of the inevitable death of the young man. The same thought is carried through into Sonnet 16, which 'replies' to Sonnet 15.

Holds in perfection stays perfect
Cheerèd and checked encouraged and rebuked
Vaunt … sap boastfully revel in their youthful vitality
inconstant transient, changing

debateth combines, conspires
sullied corrupted, dirtied
ingraft you give you life again, as a gardener grafts a cutting to make new growth

16

But wherefore do not you a mightier way
Make war upon this bloody tyrant Time,
And fortify yourself in your decay
With means more blessèd than my barren rhyme?   4
Now stand you on the top of happy hours,
And many maiden gardens, yet unset,
With virtuous wish would bear your living flowers,
Much liker than your painted counterfeit: 8
So should the lines of life that life repair
Which this time's pencil or my pupil pen
Neither in inward worth nor outward fair
Can make you live yourself in eyes of men: 12
   To give away yourself keeps yourself still,
   And you must live drawn by your own sweet skill.

The opening word, 'But', suggests that this sonnet forms a reply to the argument of the previous sonnet. It continues by saying that the ravages of Time can be more powerfully resisted through having children than through poetry. Nature is superior to art, in that children, rather than poetry, will guarantee the continuation of the young man's beauty.

The nature imagery of Sonnet 15 is continued as this sonnet argues that young women who are still virgins would willingly bear the young man's children ('maiden gardens, yet unset ... living flowers'). These natural images are contrasted with images of painting and poetry.

Many suggestions have been made for the meaning of 'lines of life' in line 9, including: pencil lines in a portrait; wrinkles showing old age; life-lines on the palm of the hand; lines of verse; or lines of a 'family tree', showing descendants. In reading the sonnet, do you think it is desirable to try to bear all these possibilities in mind, or to fix on just one meaning?

unset unplanted
painted counterfeit portrait
repair make live again
pencil small paintbrush

give away yourself marry and have children
keeps yourself still preserves you always

Who will believe my verse in time to come
If it were filled with your most high deserts?
Though yet, heaven knows, it is but as a tomb
Which hides your life, and shows not half your parts.   4
If I could write the beauty of your eyes,
And in fresh numbers number all your graces,
The age to come would say, 'This poet lies;
Such heavenly touches ne'er touched earthly faces.'   8
So should my papers (yellowed with their age)
Be scorned, like old men of less truth than tongue,
And your true rights be termed a poet's rage
And stretchèd metre of an àntique song: 12
    But were some child of yours alive that time,
    You should live twice, in it and in my rhyme.

Sonnet 17 continues the argument of the previous sonnet that poetry is less likely to convince future readers of the beauty of the young man than his children. It claims that, if only *The Sonnets* remain, future generations will disbelieve the descriptions of the young man, thinking them merely poetic exaggeration. But a child would make the young man live twice over: in the son and in *The Sonnets*.

Some of the rhymes in this sonnet are not obvious to readers today, because modern pronunciation is different from that of the first Elizabethans. For example, there are three rhymes in the sonnet which might be overlooked today:

lines 1 and 3 'come' rhymes with 'tomb' (as in 'loom')
lines 2 and 4 'deserts' rhymes with 'parts' (as in 'darts')
lines 10 and 12 'tongue' rhymes with 'song' (as in 'hung')

Try speaking the sonnet using the Elizabethan pronunciation shown above. If you were speaking the sonnet to a modern audience, would you use such pronunciation? Give reasons for your decision.

---

high deserts outstanding merits
tomb (like the inscription on a gravestone)
parts qualities, gifts
fresh numbers new verses

of less truth than tongue more talkative than truthful
true rights due praise
stretchèd metre far-fetched verse, poetic exaggeration
àntique song old-fashioned poem

Sonnets 1–17

Sonnets 1–17 form a coherent, closely integrated sequence. They urge the young man to marry to ensure that his beauty lives on. The sequence uses many analogies to support its argument. Its range of imagery includes the rose, the sun, finance and investment, music, and many other symbols which held great significance for Elizabethan readers.

The pervading theme illustrates the Renaissance doctrine of 'increase', or 'breed', namely that children guarantee the continuance of human perfection. In Greek, 'tokos' means both 'child' and 'interest on an investment'. 'Breed' carried the same meanings in Elizabethan England, where Renaissance scholarship met up with the commercialism of the age.

Many people have argued that Shakespeare's personal history can be detected in the sequence. For example, the imagery of finance and investment may hint at his interest in buying land and becoming wealthy, and at his direct experience of loans and interest.

One theory about *The Sonnets* is that Shakespeare was commissioned to write these 'breed' sonnets to persuade a young nobleman to marry. But, as he wrote them, Shakespeare came to develop a greater interest in what could be achieved in verse, and his relationship with the young man deepened into the closest of friendships. This led Shakespeare to new levels of poetic experiment, as he sought to express faithfully in verse the full range and complexity of his emotional experiences.

After the unity of theme in Sonnets 1–17, the sonnets become less of a coherent sequence from Sonnet 18 onwards. Many people have detected an unfolding story, but there are inconsistencies and puzzling breaks in the 'narrative', as Shakespeare sets down his ambivalent feelings for the young man and the dark lady.

a Look back over Sonnets 1–17 and read the closing couplet (lines 13–14) of each. Identify in each couplet the different expressions which imply 'son' or 'children'. For example, in Sonnet 1, 'the world's due'; Sonnet 2, 'thy blood'; Sonnet 3, 'thine image', and so on.

b Throughout Sonnets 1–17, Shakespeare uses a range of analogies to illustrate his theme of the need to have children. List as many as you can, then select two or three which you feel are particularly effective.

c You have been commissioned to write a sonnet urging a woman to marry and produce a daughter. Write your sonnet.

18

Shall I compare thee to a summer's day?
Thou art more lovely and more temperate:
Rough winds do shake the darling buds of May,
And summer's lease hath all too short a date;   4
Sometime too hot the eye of heaven shines,
And often is his gold complexion dimmed;
And every fair from fair sometime declines,
By chance or nature's changing course untrimmed: 8
But thy eternal summer shall not fade,
Nor lose possession of that fair thou ow'st,
Nor shall Death brag thou wand'rest in his shade,
When in eternal lines to time thou grow'st.   12
So long as men can breathe or eyes can see,
So long lives this, and this gives life to thee.

Sonnets 1–17 tried to persuade the young man to have children, thus
making sure that his beauty lives for ever. Sonnet 18 now makes the bold
claim that it is poetry that will make the young man immortal. Following
the daring assertion that the young man's loveliness surpasses that of a
summer's day, lines 3–8 describe the brevity of summer, the changeabil-
ity of the sun, and the way in which everything beautiful ('fair') will inevitably decay.

Lines 9–14 confidently claim that verse will make certain that the
young man's beauty lives as long as humanity itself. This confidence is
forcefully expressed in the emphatic monosyllables of the couplet. Such
faith in the power of poetry stands in sharp contrast to the doubt about
poetry evident in the two preceding sonnets.

Sonnet 18 has been variously described as 'sincere and emotionally
truthful', and as 'boastful and over-exaggerated'. Which description
comes closer to your own view of the sonnet?

temperate calm, even-tempered
darling lovely, young
date duration
eye of heaven sun
untrimmed robbed of beauty
(stripped of ornament)

eternal summer everlasting beauty
ow'st own, possess
eternal lines immortal verses
to time thou grow'st you and time
become one (eternal)

19

Devouring Time, blunt thou the lion's paws,
And make the earth devour her own sweet brood;
Pluck the keen teeth from the fierce tiger's jaws,
And burn the long-lived phoenix in her blood;   4
Make glad and sorry seasons as thou fleet'st,
And do whate'er thou wilt, swift-footed Time,
To the wide world and all her fading sweets;
But I forbid thee one most heinous crime: 8
O carve not with thy hours my love's fair brow,
Nor draw no lines there with thine àntique pen;
Him in thy course untainted do allow
For beauty's pattern to succeeding men.   12
   Yet do thy worst, old Time: despite thy wrong,
   My love shall in my verse ever live young.

Sonnet 19 challenges Time to exercise its most destructive powers (lines 1–7), but forbids it to spoil the young man's beauty (lines 8–12). The couplet is defiant, confident that, in the face of the worst ravages of Time, the young man's beauty will live on in *The Sonnets*.

The vivid personification of Time ('Devouring', 'swift-footed', 'old') echoes descriptions in earlier sonnets: 'never-resting time' (Sonnet 5), 'wastes of time' (Sonnet 12), 'wasteful Time' (Sonnet 15), 'bloody tyrant Time' (Sonnet 16). Because Time and its deadly effects form a major theme of Sonnets 1–126, you will find many other depictions as you read on.

For Elizabethans, the phoenix was a symbol of immortality. It was a mythical bird, which destroyed itself in fire, and rose rejuvenated from the ashes. Suggest other animal images similar to those in the first quatrain. For example, one student substituted 'unsight the eagle's eye' in line 1.

brood children, creatures
fleet'st fly, rapidly pass
fading sweets ageing but beautiful
  creatures
heinous dreadful, hateful

àntique old, grotesque
in thy course in your swift progress
untainted unspoilt
beauty's pattern as a perfect model
succeeding men future generations

20

A woman's face with Nature's own hand painted
Hast thou, the master-mistress of my passion;
A woman's gentle heart, but not acquainted
With shifting change, as is false women's fashion;   4
An eye more bright than theirs, less false in rolling,
Gilding the object whereupon it gazeth;
A man in hue, all hues in his controlling,
Which steals men's eyes and women's souls amazeth.   8
And for a woman wert thou first created,
Till Nature as she wrought thee fell a-doting,
And by addition me of thee defeated,
By adding one thing to my purpose nothing.   12
    But since she pricked thee out for women's pleasure,
    Mine be thy love, and thy love's use their treasure.

This sonnet is crucial to arguments about Shakespeare's relationship with the young man. Those who claim that it was a homosexual relationship pick out such phrases as 'master-mistress of my passion'. They stress the loving tone of this and other sonnets, and the criticism of women's love as 'shifting' and 'false'.

Those who do not believe that the relationship was homosexual focus on lines 9–14. The young man has the 'addition' of 'one thing' (a penis) which is of no interest to Shakespeare ('to my purpose nothing'). They also point out that, in Elizabethan times, it was conventional for one man to address another in ways which today would imply homosexuality.

Sonnet 20 shows that Shakespeare enjoyed a bawdy joke. He often inserted *double entendres* (sexually charged language) into his poetry and plays. Elizabethans reading the sonnets would see double meanings in lines 12–14 ('nothing' and 'treasure' were words for female genitalia; 'pricked' is an obvious pun on penis).

with Nature's own hand painted naturally beautiful, without false makeup
shifting deceitful
rolling roving, wandering
Gilding making golden
hue form, appearance, colour, complexion, shape
wrought made
fell a-doting became infatuated (went dotty)

21

So is it not with me as with that Muse,
Stirred by a painted beauty to his verse,
Who heaven itself for ornament doth use,
And every fair with his fair doth rehearse,   4
Making a couplement of proud compare
With sun and moon, with earth and sea's rich gems,
With April's first-born flowers, and all things rare
That heaven's air in this huge rondure hems.   8
O let me, true in love, but truly write,
And then believe me, my love is as fair
As any mother's child, though not so bright
As those gold candles fixed in heaven's air: 12
    Let them say more that like of hearsay well,
    I will not praise that purpose not to sell.

Shakespeare mocks other sonnet writers who overpraise their beloved by comparing their beauty with heaven, sun, moon, earth, sea, and 'all things rare'. Such comparisons are merely 'hearsay' (rumour, empty talk), exaggerating the false beauty of the beloved. In contrast, Shakespeare wishes only to write the simple truth about his love, avoiding the deceitful comparisons used by those who try to 'sell' their lover's beauty.

Experiment with reading the sonnet aloud to bring out the mocking tone of lines 1–8, expressed in both simple words ('sun', 'moon', 'earth', 'sea'), and in unfamiliar ones ('huge rondure'). Try to speak lines 9–14 as simply and sincerely as possible, but think about whether 'gold candles fixed in heaven's air' could be spoken mockingly.

Did Shakespeare himself fall into the trap of the extravagant comparisons which he is mocking here? Give your reply after reading Sonnet 18, 53 or 99.

Muse poet
Stirred inspired
painted heavily made-up
doth rehearse compares
couplement comparison, linkage

huge rondure world, universe
hems confines, contains
gold candles stars
that purpose not when I do not
  intend

22

My glass shall not persuade me I am old,
So long as youth and thou are of one date,
But when in thee time's furrows I behold,
Then look I death my days should expiate: 4
For all that beauty that doth cover thee
Is but the seemly raiment of my heart,
Which in thy breast doth live, as thine in me.
How can I then be elder than thou art?   8
O therefore, love, be of thyself so wary
As I not for myself but for thee will,
Bearing thy heart, which I will keep so chary
As tender nurse her babe from faring ill: 12
    Presume not on thy heart when mine is slain;
    Thou gav'st me thine, not to give back again.

The image of lovers exchanging their hearts develops throughout Sonnet 22. It is a symbol that they are forever part of each other, always inseparable. Shakespeare vows to keep the young man's heart safe ('so chary'), and claims that he will keep it eternally, even after death.

The sonnet is sometimes read as autobiographical, revealing that Shakespeare is older than the young man (lines 8 and 12), and that Shakespeare now wishes for death when he sees the young man growing old. Sometimes, the word 'will' in line 10 is printed as 'Will', suggesting Shakespeare's first name, rather than a declaration that the poet will be careful for his friend's sake. If you wrote out the sonnet for display or publication, would you write 'will' or 'Will'? Give reasons for your decision.

---

glass mirror
one date the same age
look I I wish, I expect
expiate end in peace
seemly raiment appropriate
  clothing

wary careful
chary tenderly, safely
faring ill harm (becoming sick)
Presume not on don't expect to get
  back

As an unperfect actor on the stage,
Who with his fear is put besides his part,
Or some fierce thing replete with too much rage,
Whose strength's abundance weakens his own heart;   4
So I, for fear of trust, forget to say
The perfect ceremony of love's rite,
And in mine own love's strength seem to decay,
O'ercharged with burthen of mine own love's might: 8
O let my looks be then the eloquence
And dumb presagers of my speaking breast,
Who plead for love, and look for recompense,
More than that tongue that more hath more expressed.   12
    O learn to read what silent love hath writ:
    To hear with eyes belongs to love's fine wit.

This sonnet expresses a distrust of the spoken word. Extreme emotion can overpower the ability to speak truly of love. Just as an actor suffering from stage fright forgets his lines, or a wild creature is disabled by excessive rage, so lack of confidence, or too much passion, reduces the power of speech and seems to weaken love.

Aware of the inadequacy of the spoken word, Shakespeare declares that his 'looks' (appearance), rather than his tongue, express his true feelings for the young man (lines 9–14).

Some people argue that Shakespeare did not, in fact, write 'looks' in line 9, but 'books'. In Shakespeare's time, 'books' meant any piece of writing, for example, *The Sonnets*. Do you think 'books' and 'looks' are equally appropriate words to use in this sonnet?

---

is put besides forgets (his lines)
replete overfull
rite ritual, what needs to be said
O'ercharged overloaded
burthen weight, burden

eloquence truthful expression
dumb presagers silent heralds, non-verbal signals
speaking breast loving heart
belongs to is the true quality of

24

Mine eye hath played the painter and hath stelled
Thy beauty's form in table of my heart;
My body is the frame wherein 'tis held,
And pèrspective it is best painter's art,   4
For through the painter must you see his skill
To find where your true image pictured lies,
Which in my bosom's shop is hanging still,
That hath his windows glazèd with thine eyes.   8
Now see what good turns eyes for eyes have done:
Mine eyes have drawn thy shape, and thine for me
Are windows to my breast, wherethrough the sun
Delights to peep, to gaze therein on thee.   12
    Yet eyes this cunning want to grace their art,
    They draw but what they see, know not the heart.

It is helpful to read Sonnet 24 bearing in mind the image of two people looking into each other's eyes. The sonnet plays with the idea of the eye as an artist, painting the beloved person and hanging the portrait in the heart ('bosom's shop').

The sonnet is deeply ambivalent, suggesting that the outward beauty of the young man may not be a true reflection of his real character. The ambivalence is implied in 'pèrspective', which could mean 'perfect picture' or 'distorted picture' (see opposite), and in 'glazèd', meaning 'clear and transparent as glass' or 'blurred and filmed over'. The doubt is made evident in the couplet, which distrusts the skill of the eyes to detect a person's true nature ('know not the heart'). Appearances can be deceptive.

stelled engraved, portrayed
table painter's board
frame picture frame
his (line 8) its (my heart's)

good turns acts of friendship
cunning skill
want lack
but (line 14) only

The Ambassadors by Holbein.

Sonnet 24 is based on a conceit (elaborate metaphor) of eyes and painting. The ambivalent image of 'pèrspective' in line 4 could refer to a picture which seems distorted when viewed from the front, but which shows a true representation when viewed from a particular angle.

In *King Richard II*, Shakespeare again uses the idea of perspectives which:

... rightly gazed upon
Show nothing but confusion, eyed awry
Distinguish form.

Holbein's painting (see above) is a famous example of a perspective picture. The curious elongated shape in the centre foreground is revealed to be a skull when viewed from one side.

Think about how the concept of 'pèrspective' as distorted portrayal relates to line 14, which suggests that appearances do not portray the real person.

25

Let those who are in favour with their stars
Of public honour and proud titles boast,
Whilst I, whom fortune of such triumph bars,
Unlooked for joy in that I honour most.   4
Great princes' favourites their fair leaves spread
But as the marigold at the sun's eye,
And in themselves their pride lies burièd,
For at a frown they in their glory die.   8
The painful warrior famousèd for fight,
After a thousand victories once foiled,
Is from the book of honour rasèd quite,
And all the rest forgot for which he toiled: 12
    Then happy I that love and am belovèd
    Where I may not remove, nor be removèd.

Sonnet 25 begins with an astrological image, claiming that some people are born lucky and enjoy great success. The poet, however, does not enjoy such 'public honour and proud titles'. Lines 5–12 show how quickly success can vanish. Just as a flower flourishes in the sunshine but closes its petals when a cloud hides the sun, so a courtier who enjoys a monarch's favour can instantly lose it, and a successful soldier can lose everything in a single defeat. The couplet makes a characteristic 'turn': Shakespeare's happiness lies in the constant love of his friend, which defies the instability of chance.

Some readers claim that lines 9–12 refer to Sir Walter Raleigh or to the Earl of Essex. Both were successful in battle, but lost the favour of Queen Elizabeth I. But it is possible that Shakespeare was generalising, and did not have a real person in mind. Is your enjoyment and understanding of the sonnet increased or decreased by trying to link it to a historical figure? (Pages 122 and 143 give other examples of similar links.)

---

in favour ... stars blessed by
  fortune
bars denies, prevents
Unlooked for unexpectedly,
  without fame
painful hard-working, much
  wounded

famousèd made famous
once foiled defeated once
rasèd quite utterly erased
remove be unfaithful
removèd dismissed

26

Lord of my love, to whom in vassalage
Thy merit hath my duty strongly knit,
To thee I send this written ambassage
To witness duty, not to show my wit;   4
Duty so great, which wit so poor as mine
May make seem bare, in wanting words to show it,
But that I hope some good conceit of thine
In thy soul's thought (all naked) will bestow it,   8
Till whatsoever star that guides my moving
Points on me graciously with fair aspèct,
And puts apparel on my tottered loving,
To show me worthy of thy sweet respect: 12
    Then may I dare to boast how I do love thee,
    Till then, not show my head where thou mayst prove me.

The vocabulary of Sonnet 26 emphasises the obligations which Shakespeare felt he owed to a social superior: 'Lord', 'vassalage', 'Duty so great'. Shakespeare stresses his low social status, as he did in Sonnet 25, line 3. He also seems to emphasise his lack of skill in writing poetry: 'wit so poor as mine', 'bare', 'wanting (lacking) words', 'all naked'. He hopes that his guiding star will eventually smile on him. Until that time, he dares not declare his love.

Some students find the sonnet's tone excessively submissive. But perhaps Shakespeare was simply using the language considered conventional when an Elizabethan poet was writing to a potential patron. To test your own view, try two 'thought experiments':

a Imagine that you are speaking the sonnet kneeling down, addressing someone you see as a social superior.

b Imagine that you are standing face to face with a social equal.

  What differences do you notice in your two readings?

---

vassalage servitude, loyalty	**conceit** opinion, thought
knit bound in service	**all naked** without prejudice
ambassage message, sonnet	**moving** life, actions
wit intelligence	**tottered loving** poor verses
wanting lacking	**prove** test

Weary with toil, I haste me to my bed,
The dear repose for limbs with travel tired,
But then begins a journey in my head
To work my mind, when body's work's expired;   4
For then my thoughts (from far where I abide)
Intend a zealous pilgrimage to thee,
And keep my drooping eyelids open wide,
Looking on darkness which the blind do see;   8
Save that my soul's imaginary sight
Presents thy shadow to my sightless view,
Which like a jewel (hung in ghastly night)
Makes black night beauteous, and her old face new.   12
    Lo thus by day my limbs, by night my mind,
    For thee, and for myself, no quiet find.

Sonnets 27 and 28 explore the theme of sleeplessness. Shakespeare seems to be far away from the young man (perhaps touring with an acting company?). The two sonnets describe how the young man is always in Shakespeare's thoughts, bringing him both comfort and sorrow.

Both sonnets are full of antitheses (see page 188) or contrasts, which are often expressed in the same line: 'weary'/'haste', 'repose'/'tired', 'mind'/'body', 'drooping'/'open', and so on. The twisting and turning antitheses help to convey the restlessness of a person who cannot sleep. His body is weary, but his imagination, full of thoughts of his loved one, keeps him awake, and he finds no quiet in sleep.

Try reading the two sonnets as a sequence, making a twenty-eight line poem. You will find that they not only have a common theme, but are also linked by repeated words, shared rhymes and symmetrical structures.

dear repose sweet rest
expired finished
abide lodge, reside
Intend set out on

zealous pilgrimage loving and
   devoted journey
Save that except that
imaginary sight imagination
ghastly ghostly, terrifying

How can I then return in happy plight
That am debarred the benefit of rest?
When day's oppression is not eased by night,
But day by night and night by day oppressed;   4
And each (though enemies to either's reign)
Do in consent shake hands to torture me,
The one by toil, the other to complain
How far I toil, still farther off from thee.   8
I tell the day to please him thou art bright,
And dost him grace when clouds do blot the heaven;
So flatter I the swart-complexioned night,
When sparkling stars twire not thou gild'st the even: 12
 But day doth daily draw my sorrows longer,
 And night doth nightly make griefs' length seem stronger.

Sonnet 28 continues the theme of the previous sonnet, namely the rest-lessness and dejection of someone who cannot sleep. Throughout the sonnet, Shakespeare describes how day and night combine to oppress him. He tries to appease them by claiming that the young man brightens and beautifies both day and night. But his efforts are not convincing, and continued absence from the young man only deepens his sorrows.

To experience the way in which the sonnet creates a mood of weari-ness and tedium, read line 4, bringing out the sense of fatigued monotony by emphasising 'day' and 'night' in 'day by night and night by day op-pressed'. Then consider why line 14 seems longer than other lines in the sonnet, conveying the sense that the night will never end.

Decide whether you think that both sonnets share the same tone, or whether the mood changes from line to line, or from quatrain to quatrain.

---

happy plight cheerful state, good condition
debarred forbidden, denied
shake hands agree, unite
dost him grace make him beautiful

swart-complexioned dark-faced
twire peep, twinkle
gild'st the even make the evening golden

29

When in disgrace with Fortune and men's eyes,
I all alone beweep my outcast state,
And trouble deaf heaven with my bootless cries,
And look upon myself and curse my fate, 4
Wishing me like to one more rich in hope,
Featured like him, like him with friends possessed,
Desiring this man's art, and that man's scope,
With what I most enjoy contented least; 8
Yet in these thoughts myself almost despising,
Haply I think on thee, and then my state
(Like to the lark at break of day arising
From sullen earth) sings hymns at heaven's gate; 12
    For thy sweet love rememb'red such wealth brings
    That then I scorn to change my state with kings.

Sonnet 29 describes how Shakespeare's 'outcast state' (melancholy sense of low status and worthlessness) changes to joy when he thinks of his friend. He thinks himself a worldly failure; his luck ('Fortune') has run out, and he feels despised by others. He envies other men for their looks, friends, abilities and opportunities. But thoughts of his own friend bring such intense joy and consolation that he would not change places with anyone, however appealing their situation might seem.

a Compare the mood of lines 1–8 with the mood of lines 9–14.

b There is much uncertainty about line 8. What was it that Shakespeare most enjoyed but which now gives him little pleasure: his acting? his writing? Whatever it was, do you feel that the line expresses a familiar experience of a depressed person?

c The sonnet is a single sentence. Suggest where you think pauses could be most appropriately placed if it were spoken aloud.

---

in disgrace out of favour
bootless useless
Featured handsome
art skill, learning

scope abilities, opportunities, achievements, freedom
Haply fortunately, by chance
state (line 10) state of mind
state (line 14) social status

When to the sessions of sweet silent thought
I summon up remembrance of things past,
I sigh the lack of many a thing I sought,
And with old woes new wail my dear time's waste;   4
Then can I drown an eye (unused to flow)
For precious friends hid in death's dateless night,
And weep afresh love's long since cancelled woe,
And moan th'expense of many a vanished sight;   8
Then can I grieve at grievances foregone,
And heavily from woe to woe tell o'er
The sad account of fore-bemoanèd moan,
Which I new pay as if not paid before: 12
   But if the while I think on thee (dear friend)
   All losses are restored, and sorrows end.

The 'compensation' theme of Sonnet 29 is continued here. However sad Shakespeare may be, his melancholy ends when he thinks of his friend. However, the structure of Sonnet 30 differs from that of the previous sonnet. Here, lines 1–12 express sorrow, and the 'turn' (change of mood) comes in the couplet, lines 13–14.

Running through the sonnet is the image of a court of law in which compensation is finally obtained. There are many legal or financial implications: 'sessions', 'summon', 'dateless', 'cancelled', 'expense', 'grievances', 'account', 'pay', 'losses', 'restored'.

This sonnet has been compared to slow mournful music, as its effect is heightened by the use of alliteration and by the repetition of vowel sounds. Try reading the sonnet in order to bring out its sorrow for past failures, irrecoverable time, and dead friends. In your first reading, stress the alliterative words (those which begin with the same letter). Then read it again without such emphasis, but with its effect in mind.

---

sessions meetings of a law court
summon up call up, order to appear
unused to flow not usually tearful
dateless endless

heavily sadly
tell o'er count up
fore-bemoanèd moan old griefs, past mournings

31

Thy bosom is endearèd with all hearts,
Which I by lacking have supposèd dead,
And there reigns love and all love's loving parts,
And all those friends which I thought burièd.   4
How many a holy and obsequious tear
Hath dear religious love stol'n from mine eye,
As interest of the dead, which now appear
But things removed that hidden in thee lie!   8
Thou art the grave where buried love doth live,
Hung with the trophies of my lovers gone,
Who all their parts of me to thee did give;
That due of many now is thine alone.   12
    Their images I loved I view in thee,
    And thou (all they) hast all the all of me.

Sonnet 31 seems to reveal that the 'losses' of Sonnet 30 are dead friends. Lines 5–8 of each sonnet tell of tears shed for friends who have died. Using imagery based on the rituals of the Christian burial service, Sonnet 31 offers comfort, saying that all past friends are now part of the young man, and their qualities live on in his beauty. As a result, the young man now receives all the love which Shakespeare once felt for his friends.

As you read the sonnet notice:

a All the words which refer to religion, death and burial.

b The seven repetitions of 'all'. What quality do you think the repeated use of 'all' gives to the sonnet?

c The echoes of Sonnet 30. Try reading the two sonnets in sequence to discover if you feel that, in Sonnet 31, 'all losses are restored' as Shakespeare thinks of the young man.

---

bosom breast, heart
endearèd with loved by, made precious by
lacking not having
obsequious grieving, dutiful

interest due, right
trophies emblems, memorials (hung on tombs to record the qualities of the dead person)

32

If thou survive my well-contented day,
When that churl Death my bones with dust shall cover,
And shalt by fortune once more re-survey
These poor rude lines of thy deceasèd lover,   4
Compare them with the bett'ring of the time,
And though they be outstripped by every pen,
Reserve them for my love, not for their rhyme,
Exceeded by the height of happier men.   8
O then vouchsafe me but this loving thought:
'Had my friend's Muse grown with this growing age,
A dearer birth than this his love had brought
To march in ranks of better equipage: 12
    But since he died, and poets better prove,
    Theirs for their style I'll read, his for his love.'

Shakespeare imagines that, after his death, his friend may read *The Sonnets* again. Shakespeare assesses his own poetry as being of little worth, 'These poor rude lines'. He acknowledges that he will be outclassed by other poets ('outstripped by every pen'), and appeals to the young man to read *The Sonnets* for the sincerity of the loving friendship which they depict. They may be inferior to others in poetic style, but they speak truthfully.

Shakespeare seems well aware that he was living in an age of remarkable developments in poetry, 'this growing age' (see page 178). He hopes that the young man will think that, if he (Shakespeare) had lived, his verses would rank equal with the best poetry of later times ('march in ranks of better equipage').

Did Shakespeare write Sonnet 32 with his tongue in his cheek, with ironic modesty? Compare his description of his poetry as 'poor rude lines' with his description of it in Sonnet 18, line 12.

---

well-contented day welcome day of death
churl surly ruffian
fortune chance
re-survey read again
rude lines awkward sonnets
bett'ring superior poems

outstripped by every pen inferior to other poets' sonnets
vouchsafe grant
Muse poetic ability
equipage equipment (poetry) of equal worth

33

Full many a glorious morning have I seen
Flatter the mountain tops with sovereign eye,
Kissing with golden face the meadows green,
Gilding pale streams with heavenly alcumy,   4
Anon permit the basest clouds to ride
With ugly rack on his celestial face,
And from the fòrlorn world his visage hide,
Stealing unseen to west with this disgrace: 8
Even so my sun one early morn did shine
With all triumphant splendour on my brow;
But out alack, he was but one hour mine,
The region cloud hath masked him from me now.   12
   Yet him for this my love no whit disdaineth:
   Suns of the world may stain, when heaven's sun staineth.

A new theme is introduced, that of estrangement. Just as clouds hide the sun, so the relationship between Shakespeare and the young man is now under a cloud. Lines 9–12 suggest that a brief period of glorious friendship is now over, ended by 'The region cloud'.

The sonnet hints at disgrace from a wrongdoing: 'basest', 'ugly', 'Stealing', 'disgrace', 'stain'. But the couplet declares that Shakespeare's love is unchanged ('no whit disdaineth'): just as the sun may be briefly dimmed by clouds, so may the 'Suns (sons) of the world'.

A sense of unease pervades the sonnet. For example, 'alcumy' (alchemy, line 4) was a false science which claimed to turn base metals into gold. Do you think the sonnet implies that the sun and the young man also exercise false magic? What is the source of the young man's disgrace ('region cloud') that has come between the two friends? You will find further evidence of Shakespeare's troubled mind in the sonnets which follow.

Full very
Flatter make beautiful, delude
sovereign eye the sun
Gilding making golden
Anon soon
basest least worthy, inferior

rack clouds
celestial heavenly
visage face
out alack alas
no whit not at all

34

Why didst thou promise such a beauteous day,
And make me travel forth without my cloak,
To let base clouds o'ertake me in my way,
Hiding thy brav'ry in their rotten smoke? 4
'Tis not enough that through the cloud thou break,
To dry the rain on my storm-beaten face,
For no man well of such a salve can speak,
That heals the wound, and cures not the disgrace: 8
Nor can thy shame give physic to my grief;
Though thou repent, yet I have still the loss:
Th'offender's sorrow lends but weak relief
To him that bears the strong offence's cross. 12
    Ah, but those tears are pearl which thy love sheeds,
    And they are rich, and ransom all ill deeds.

The anguish at betrayed friendship, which was evident in Sonnet 33, continues here. The image of the sun hidden by 'base clouds' is once again used as a metaphor for the shadow cast over the relationship between the poet and his friend. Some 'strong offence' (dishonourable wrongdoing) has brought disgrace on Shakespeare and shame to the young man.

In lines 5–12, Shakespeare refuses to be comforted by his friend's repentant attempts at consolation; the feeling of disgrace remains. But the couplet seems to reveal that comfort is possible: the young man's precious tears of love make amends for the wrong he has done.

The sonnet employs many metaphors: weather, travelling, medicine, the cross of Christ, pearls, ransom. Suggest several ways in which each metaphor conveys more than its literal meaning. For example, 'travel forth' is a metaphor of journeying. It could refer to trustful friendship, to Shakespeare's theatrical career, and to mixing with the young man's friends.

base ignoble, inferior	**cross** burden, suffering
brav'ry splendour, finery	**pearl** like precious jewels
salve medicine	**sheeds** sheds (weeps)
give physic to cure	**ransom** atone for, compensate

No more be grieved at that which thou hast done:
Roses have thorns, and silver fountains mud,
Clouds and eclipses stain both moon and sun,
And loathsome canker lives in sweetest bud.   4
All men make faults, and even I in this,
Authòrising thy trespass with compare,
Myself corrupting salving thy amiss,
Excusing thy sins more than their sins are;   8
For to thy sensual fault I bring in sense –
Thy adverse party is thy advocate –
And 'gainst myself a lawful plea commence:
Such civil war is in my love and hate   12
　　That I an àccessary needs must be
　　To that sweet thief which sourly robs from me.

Sonnet 35 excuses the young man's faults by acknowledging that all beautiful things have blemishes. In line 6, Shakespeare describes his own defect as 'compare' or making poetic comparisons (with roses, fountains, and so on). Such sophistry (word-juggling) is corrupting. It uses 'sense' (reason) to make the young man's 'sensual fault' (offence) seem greater than it is.

Legal imagery runs through the sonnet: 'trespass', 'amiss', 'adverse party', 'advocate', 'lawful plea', 'commence' (begin a legal case), 'àccessary', 'thief'. Shakespeare sees himself as both prosecuting and defending counsel for the young man. This ambivalence is made clear in the couplet, with its contrast of 'sweet' and 'sourly'.

A modern critic wrote of line 12, 'a lesser poet would have written "tween"'. Suggest why the choice of 'in' as opposed to 'tween' (between) makes this a better sonnet.

stain dim, corrupt	**amiss** fault
canker cankerworm (which destroys the flower)	**bring in** apply, introduce
	sense reason
Authòrising justifying	**adverse party** opponent
trespass offence	**advocate** defence lawyer
salving condoning, excusing	**àccessary** accomplice

Let me confess that we two must be twain,
Although our undivided loves are one:
So shall those blots that do with me remain,
Without thy help, by me be borne alone.   4
In our two loves there is but one respect,
Though in our lives a separable spite,
Which though it alter not love's sole effect,
Yet doth it steal sweet hours from love's delight.   8
I may not evermore acknowledge thee,
Lest my bewailèd guilt should do thee shame,
Nor thou with public kindness honour me,
Unless thou take that honour from thy name: 12
    But do not so; I love thee in such sort,
    As thou being mine, mine is thy good report.

The theme of estrangement in Sonnets 33, 34 and 35 continues as Sonnet
36 tells of the 'blots' (disgraces) and 'guilt' which divide the two friends.
Shakespeare declares that he alone must bear the burden of 'those blots'.
He must not be seen as the young man's friend, for fear of shaming him
and lowering his 'report' (reputation).

The problem of treating *The Sonnets* as autobiographical (see pages
3–4) is evident here. For instance, what is the 'guilt' referred to in line 10?
But whether or not Shakespeare is drawing on his personal experience,
this sonnet displays his poetic power. For example, the use of 'respect' in
line 5 shows how a single word conjures up a wealth of possible meanings
which enrich interpretation: 'concern', 'aim', 'status', 'motive', 'regard',
'reference' or 'care'.

How is your response to the sonnet affected by reading it together with
Sonnets 33, 34 and 35 as explorations of a common theme?

---

twain two different persons, parted
separable spite cruel separation
  (causing spite), dividing cruelty
  (caused by spite)
sole effect uniting power

acknowledge thee show that I
  know you
bewailèd guilt weeping for shame,
  obvious signs of guilt
public kindness obvious familiarity
take that honour remove honour

37

As a decrepit father takes delight
To see his active child do deeds of youth,
So I, made lame by Fortune's dearest spite,
Take all my comfort of thy worth and truth;   4
For whether beauty, birth, or wealth, or wit,
Or any of these all, or all, or more,
Intitled in thy parts, do crownèd sit,
I make my love ingrafted to this store: 8
So then I am not lame, poor, nor despised,
Whilst that this shadow doth such substance give,
That I in thy abundance am sufficed,
And by a part of all thy glory live: 12
    Look what is best, that best I wish in thee;
    This wish I have, then ten times happy me.

This sonnet expresses the idea of compensation (see page 39), a recurring theme of *The Sonnets*. Shakespeare regrets his bad luck, but takes great comfort from thinking about the young man's successes and qualities.

The sonnet claims that, just as an enfeebled father gains pleasure from watching his active child, so Shakespeare derives all his comfort and satisfaction from the young man's glorious and abundant excellences. Bad luck ('Fortune's dearest spite') has crippled him, but he is restored by calling up the young man's image ('shadow') in his mind. He draws strength from being 'ingrafted to' (attached to and nourished by) the young man's 'store' (many perfections).

The word 'lame' has sometimes been taken literally, rather than seen as a metaphor for someone oppressed by bad luck. Using this sonnet and Sonnet 89, some people claim that Shakespeare was physically lame. Do you think that this claim is justified, or merely fanciful? Give reasons for your reply.

---

decrepit old and weak	**birth** inherited high status
Fortune luck	**Intitled** listed
dearest spite direct malice, most grievous cruelty	**sufficed** satisfied
	Look what whatever

How can my Muse want subject to invent
While thou dost breathe, that pour'st into my verse
Thine own sweet argument, too excellent
For every vulgar paper to rehearse?   4
O give thyself the thanks if aught in me
Worthy perusal stand against thy sight,
For who's so dumb that cannot write to thee,
When thou thyself dost give invention light?   8
Be thou the tenth Muse, ten times more in worth
Than those old nine which rhymers invocate,
And he that calls on thee, let him bring forth
Eternal numbers to outlive long date.   12
    If my slight Muse do please these curious days,
    The pain be mine, but thine shall be the praise.

Sonnet 38 flatters the young man as the inspiration and subject ('argument') of *The Sonnets*. The mood is one of self-deprecation, as Shakespeare plays down his own poetic ability, and credits anything worth reading in *The Sonnets* to the young man. Who could fail to write poetry when inspired by him?

In lines 1 and 13, 'Muse' probably implies 'ability to write poetry'. In lines 9–10, the reference is to the nine muses, the mythical goddesses who inspired learning and artistic creation. The young man is imagined to be the 'tenth Muse', worth much more than all the others.

Some readers feel that Sonnet 38 is insincere in its flattery. However, many poets followed the convention of using hyperbole (exaggeration) and compliment to gain favour with a patron. In *As You Like It*, one character says of another's flattery, 'That was laid on with a trowel' (huge and obvious flattery). Do you think that this phrase is appropriate to the sonnet as well?

---

want lack
vulgar paper ordinary poem
rehearse repeat
aught anything
perusal reading
invention imagination

rhymers poets
invocate invoke
numbers verses
curious critical, experimental
pain effort

39

O how thy worth with manners may I sing,
When thou art all the better part of me?
What can mine own praise to mine own self bring?
And what is't but mine own when I praise thee? 4
Even for this, let us divided live,
And our dear love lose name of single one,
That by this separation I may give
That due to thee which thou deserv'st alone. 8
O absence, what a torment wouldst thou prove,
Were it not thy sour leisure gave sweet leave
To entertain the time with thoughts of love,
Which time and thoughts so sweetly dost deceive, 12
    And that thou teachest how to make one twain,
    By praising him here who doth hence remain.

Shakespeare argues that, in praising his friend, he is actually praising himself, because their love makes them one person (lines 1–4). Only by being apart can rightful praise be given. Separation ('absence') would give Shakespeare welcome time to think about his friend, and would restore unity ('make one twain'). Although the friend is physically absent, he is 'here', in Shakespeare's heart (line 14).

Sonnet 39 is less familiar than many other sonnets, perhaps because of its lack of imagery and of its intricate, abstract argument. Nevertheless, it uses very familiar language, and its theme of unity in separation echoes other sonnets.

Do you agree that the sonnet expresses each of the following proverbs?

'Absence makes the heart grow fonder.'
'A friend is one's second self.'
'Self-praise is no recommendation.'

---

manners modesty
Even for because of
name of single one the reputation of unity
due rightful reward

sour leisure unwelcome free time
sweet leave pleasing permission
entertain pass
dost deceive beguile, make pleasant
doth hence remain is far away

40

Take all my loves, my love, yea, take them all;
What hast thou then more than thy hadst before?
No love, my love, that thou mayst true love call;
All mine was thine, before thou hadst this more.   4
Then if for my love thou my love receivest,
I cannot blame thee for my love thou usest;
But yet be blamed, if thou this self deceivest
By wilful taste of what thy self refusest.   8
I do forgive thy robb'ry, gentle thief,
Although thou steal thee all my poverty;
And yet love knows it is a greater grief
To bear love's wrong than hate's known injury.   12
     Lascivious grace, in whom all ill well shows,
     Kill me with spites, yet we must not be foes.

Sonnets 40, 41 and 42 express Shakespeare's feelings at knowing that his friend has stolen his mistress (who is the main subject of Sonnets 127–52). The young man's treachery is forgiven (line 9), but bitterness and resentment seem to be the dominant mood. The sonnet is filled with ambiguities, for example in its oxymorons: 'gentle thief', 'Lascivious grace', 'ill well'. The following summary of the sonnet is only one possible interpretation:

> Take my love and my mistress, but don't imagine that you now possess more love than before. If you love her for my sake, I cannot blame you, but you are to be blamed for enjoying sex yet refusing to marry. I forgive you your treachery, although it hurts me more because you are a friend, not an enemy. Your beauty hides evil. Your treachery is hurtful, but I cannot be your enemy.

In what tone would you speak line 1: angry, resigned, submissive, spiteful, or in some other way?

---

usest have sex with
wilful taste lustful enjoyment
what thy self refusest (that is, marriage, see Sonnets 1–17)
steal thee take for yourself

all my poverty everything I have
Lascivious grace lustful beauty
all ill well shows evil looks beautiful
spites malicious behaviour

41

Those pretty wrongs that liberty commits,
When I am sometime absent from thy heart,
Thy beauty and thy years full well befits,
For still temptation follows where thou art.   4
Gentle thou art, and therefore to be won,
Beauteous thou art, therefore to be assailed;
And when a woman woos, what woman's son
Will sourly leave her till he have prevailed?   8
Ay me, but yet thou mightst my seat forbear,
And chide thy beauty and thy straying youth,
Who lead thee in their riot even there
Where thou art forced to break a twofold truth: 12
    Hers, by thy beauty tempting her to thee,
    Thine, by thy beauty being false to me.

Sonnet 41 continues the theme of Sonnet 40: Shakespeare's betrayal by his friend who has taken up with his mistress. At first, it seems to excuse the young man by blaming youth and beauty, but the closing couplet is blunt in its accusation.

Lines 1–4 admit that sexual misbehaviour ('pretty wrongs') is natural for handsome young men. Lines 5–8 make the woman an active partner: she has invited seduction by the young man. But lines 9–14 are reproachful in tone, saying that the friend could have left Shakespeare's mistress alone ('my seat forbear'). He has been doubly unfaithful, to the woman *and* to Shakespeare.

Try a reading of the sonnet making lines 1–8 calm, tolerant of the young man's fickleness. For example, 'pretty wrongs' could be spoken as a friendly joke ('pretty' = slight, attractive). Make lines 9–14 quite different in tone, accusing and reproachful. Then suggest your own view of the sonnet's tone, and how it could be spoken.

---

liberty sexual misconduct
befits is appropriate to
still always
Gentle kind-hearted, a gentleman
assailed seduced

prevailed succeeded
chide rebuke
straying unfaithful
riot debauchery, misbehaviour
truth troth, promise

'Unknown lady' by Isaac Oliver.

Sonnets 40, 41 and 42 introduce a 'love triangle' which will be explored in more depth in Sonnets 127–54. They concern the woman who has become known as the 'dark lady' of *The Sonnets*. She seems to have been Shakespeare's mistress, and her love affair with the young man caused Shakespeare great mental torment.

No one knows who the dark lady was, but you can find some suggestions about her identity on pages 147–8. The subject of this picture, painted somewhere between 1595 and 1600, is also unknown.

That thou hast her, it is not all my grief,
And yet it may be said I loved her dearly;
That she hath thee is of my wailing chief,
A loss in love that touches me more nearly.   4
Loving offenders, thus I will excuse ye:
Thou dost love her because thou know'st I love her,
And for my sake even so doth she abuse me,
Suff'ring my friend for my sake to approve her.   8
If I lose thee, my loss is my love's gain,
And losing her, my friend hath found that loss;
Both find each other, and I lose both twain,
And both for my sake lay on me this cross.   12
    But here's the joy, my friend and I are one.
    Sweet flattery! then she loves but me alone.

Shakespeare seems to be making the best of a hopeless situation as he gathers up here the themes of Sonnets 36–41, namely betrayed friendship and the 'one-ness' of friends. His friend and his mistress have both betrayed him, but he tries to cheer himself with the delusion ('Sweet flattery!') that she still loves him, because he and his friend are one. Use the following summary to help you with the sonnet:

> My main sorrow is not you having her, but her having you. However, I excuse you both, because it is for my love that you both offended. My losing both of you means that you both gain, causing me suffering. Therefore, I cheerfully delude myself: my unity in love with my friend means that she loves me!

Work with two other students, and take parts as Shakespeare, the friend and the woman. Read the sonnet aloud. Each time a person is mentioned or implied, everyone points emphatically to that person. There are well over forty such references.

---

of my wailing chief the major reason for my sorrow
touches affects
nearly deeply
Suff'ring allowing

approve seduce, love
both twain both of you
cross suffering (echoing the Crucifixion)
flattery deception

43

When most I wink, then do mine eyes best see,
For all the day they view things unrespected;
But when I sleep, in dreams they look on thee,
And darkly bright, are bright in dark directed.   4
Then thou, whose shadow shadows doth make bright,
How would thy shadow's form form happy show
To the clear day with thy much clearer light,
When to unseeing eyes thy shade shines so!   8
How would (I say) mine eyes be blessèd made,
By looking on thee in the living day,
When in dead night thy fair imperfect shade
Through heavy sleep on sightless eyes doth stay!   12
    All days are nights to see till I see thee,
    And nights bright days when dreams do show thee me.

Sonnet 43 links sleep and dreams with sight and darkness. Daylight presents only ordinary things to view (line 2), but night brings sleep, and sleep brings dreams. In dreams, the image of the friend outshines all else, making darkness bright.

The sonnet uses repetitions and antitheses to create paradoxes. The contrast set up in the first line (when I close my eyes, I see best) continues throughout the sonnet. For example, 'darkly bright' and 'bright in dark' (line 4); 'living day', 'dead night' (lines 10 and 11). Words and phrases are reflected, as if in a mirror, but often with different meanings ('shadow shadows', 'form form'). Things are not what they seem: eyes can be 'unseeing' and 'sightless'.

Think about the following pairs of contrasts as you read the sonnet: dreaming/waking, night/day, light/dark, seeing/unseeing, shadow/substance. Does one pair of contrasts strike you as being more dominant than the others?

---

wink sleep, close my eyes
unrespected unimportant, without interest
shadow shadows image darkness
shadow's form body

form happy show make a wonderful sight
shade image
blessèd fortunate, favoured by God
fair imperfect shade beautiful insubstantial image

44

If the dull substance of my flesh were thought,
Injurious distance should not stop my way,
For then despite of space I would be brought,
From limits far remote, where thou dost stay.   4
No matter then although my foot did stand
Upon the farthest earth removed from thee,
For nimble thought can jump both sea and land
As soon as think the place where he would be.   8
But ah, thought kills me that I am not thought,
To leap large lengths of miles when thou art gone,
But that, so much of earth and water wrought,
I must attend time's leisure with my moan,   12
    Receiving nought by elements so slow
    But heavy tears, badges of either's woe.

Sonnets 44 and 45 contain an extended image of the doctrine of the four elements, an ancient belief that all matter was made up of earth, water, fire and air. Sonnet 44 is based on two of the elements, earth and water, the 'dull substance' of line 1. They were thought to be heavy, slow and ignoble.

Shakespeare wishes that his body were like thought, able to fly anywhere in an instant to be with his friend ('For nimble thought can jump both sea and land'). Realising that he is separated from his beloved by those same elements ('sea and land' = water and earth), he weeps the 'heavy tears' of earth and water.

Just as 'thought' is personified, so, too, is 'time'. Line 12 imagines time as a monarch who keeps a sorrowful subject waiting ('attend time's leisure').

You may find it helpful to read Sonnets 44 and 45 together as one twenty-eight line poem.

dull substance heavy material (earth and water)	**wrought** composed, made
Injurious spiteful, cruel, unjust	**attend time's leisure** wait patiently
limits far remote distant places	**moan** sadness
my foot did stand I happened to be	**either's** earth's and water's

45

The other two, slight air and purging fire,
Are both with thee, wherever I abide;
The first my thought, the other my desire,
These present-absent with swift motion slide;   4
For when these quicker elements are gone
In tender embassy of love to thee,
My life, being made of four, with two alone
Sinks down to death, oppressed with melancholy,   8
Until life's composition be recured
By those swift messengers returned from thee,
Who even but now come back again assured
Of thy fair health, recounting it to me.   12
    This told, I joy, but then no longer glad,
    I send them back again and straight grow sad.

The image of the four elements begun in Sonnet 44 continues here. Shakespeare imagines his thoughts as air, and his desire as fire. Both are his 'swift messengers', always with his friend. But, left with only earth and water, the poet cannot live, as he is oppressed by the dullness of sorrow and melancholy. Only the balance of all four elements can restore him to health.

Line 4 contains one of the most striking paradoxes in the whole sonnet sequence, 'present-absent'. How can thought and desire be in two places at once, simultaneously with Shakespeare and his friend? How can they be both 'present' and 'absent' at the same time? Think about your response to the following claim:

> 'Present-absent' is Shakespeare's quantum theory: the possibility of
> being both a wave and a particle at the same time. It can't really be so, but
> such imaginative leaps are part of the essence of poetry, physically
> impossible, but imaginatively and emotionally true.

---

slight insubstantial
purging cleansing, purifying
abide stay
slide journey, move
tender embassy loving journey

life's composition (that is: earth, air, fire and water)
recured restored to health
swift messengers air and fire
recounting telling

Mine eye and heart are at a mortal war,
How to divide the conquest of thy sight:
Mine eye my heart thy picture's sight would bar,
My heart mine eye the freedom of that right.   4
My heart doth plead that thou in him dost lie
(A closet never pierced with crystal eyes),
But the defendant doth that plea deny,
And says in him thy fair appearance lies.   8
To 'cide this title is impanellèd
A quest of thoughts, all tenants to the heart,
And by their verdict is determinèd
The clear eye's moiety and the dear heart's part,   12
    As thus: mine eye's due is thy outward part,
    And my heart's right thy inward love of heart.

Sonnets 46 and 47 are closely linked. Both address the conflict between the eye and the heart, the relationship between outward appearance and inward qualities. This contrast between infatuation with physical beauty, and sincere love of inner moral character, was a favourite topic for poets in Shakespeare's time.

The sonnet imagines that the eye and the heart are in dispute over the eye's refusal to let the heart see the loved one. They have taken the case to court to decide who has the better claim. Legal imagery predominates: 'bar', 'right', 'plead', 'defendant', 'plea', 'impanellèd', 'quest', 'verdict'.

Is it the eye or the heart which comes off best in the verdict expressed in lines 13–14? Or does the verdict fail to resolve the 'mortal war' between eye and heart?

---

mortal deadly
bar prohibit
closet box, small private room
crystal clear, unclouded
'cide decide

impanellèd enrolled on a jury
quest inquest
tenants to supporters of
moiety portion

Betwixt mine eye and heart a league is took,
And each doth good turns now unto the other:
When that mine eye is famished for a look,
Or heart in love with sighs himself doth smother,   4
With my love's picture then my eye doth feast,
And to the painted banquet bids my heart;
Another time mine eye is my heart's guest,
And in his thoughts of love doth share a part.   8
So either by thy picture or my love,
Thyself, away, are present still with me,
For thou not farther than my thoughts canst move,
And I am still with them, and they with thee;   12
   Or if they sleep, thy picture in my sight
   Awakes my heart to heart's and eye's delight.

The exploration of the relationship of eye and heart continues. In the previous sonnet they were at war, fighting each other in court. In Sonnet 47, they reach an agreement ('league') to help each other. The central image is that of eating. The eye allows the heart to enjoy the portrait of the young man, and the heart allows the eye to share its 'thoughts of love'. In this way, both heart and eye can be satisfied.

Critics have been very severe in judging the quality of Sonnets 46 and 47. One said that they 'evoke a sense of futile waste, of barren ingenuity, and of neurotic diversion of energy on to trivia'. In other words, Shakespeare was just idly playing with language.

You don't have to believe the critics. It is far better to make up your own mind about the poetic worth of the two sonnets. Think about whether you consider the sonnets to be simply clever and ingenious exercises, or whether they feel sincere, expressing 'true' emotions.

---

league is took treaty of friendship is made
good turns help
famished starved

smother depress
painted banquet enjoyment of the portrait
still always

48

How careful was I, when I took my way,
Each trifle under truest bars to thrust,
That to my use it might un-usèd stay
From hands of falsehood, in sure wards of trust!   4
But thou, to whom my jewels trifles are,
Most worthy comfort, now my greatest grief,
Thou best of dearest, and mine only care,
Art left the prey of every vulgar thief.   8
Thee have I not locked up in any chest,
Save where thou art not, though I feel thou art,
Within the gentle closure of my breast,
From whence at pleasure thou mayst come and part;   12
    And even thence thou wilt be stol'n, I fear,
    For truth proves thievish for a prize so dear.

About to leave on a journey, Shakespeare locks up his trifling possessions to protect them from thieving hands ('hands of falsehood'). But he fears that, while he is away, someone will steal something far more precious, namely his friend's affection. He tries to find comfort in the thought that his friend is kept safely in his heart. However, the couplet expresses the fear that honesty itself ('truth') will become a thief of such precious beauty.

In lines 6–7, the antitheses suggest that Shakespeare has very contradictory feelings for his friend: 'comfort'/'grief', 'dearest'/'care'. The two lines express the mixed emotions experienced by someone parting for a long time from the person they love. Do you think that line 10 shows that Shakespeare really knows he has lost the young man's love?

took my way left on a journey
trifle unimportant thing
truest bars safest locks
sure wards safe prisons ('ward' = notches to make a key fit a lock)
dearest what is most loved

care sorrow
chest box, breast
Save except
part depart
truth honesty

49

Against that time (if ever that time come)
When I shall see thee frown on my defècts,
Whenas thy love hath cast his utmost sum,
Called to that audit by advised respects;   4
Against that time when thou shalt strangely pass,
And scarcely greet me with that sun, thine eye,
When love converted from the thing it was
Shall reasons find of settled gravity: 8
Against that time do I insconce me here
Within the knowledge of mine own desert,
And this my hand against myself uprear,
To guard the lawful reasons on thy part.   12
    To leave poor me thou hast the strength of laws,
    Since why to love I can allege no cause.

Shakespeare thinks ahead to a time when his friend's love will have cooled. A financial metaphor in lines 3–4 envisages the time when the friend has closed the account of love or 'cast his utmost sum' (that is, added up the final total and closed the account). The repetition of the same phrase, 'Against that time' (in preparation for the time), at the beginning of each quatrain, may suggest Shakespeare's anxiety.

There are sharply differing interpretations of lines 9–14, which describe how Shakespeare will react in the future to being treated like a stranger. Does he lift his hand to protect himself against the accusations of his friend ('guard' = guard against)? Or does he lift his hand to swear as witness against himself ('guard' = swear to protect)?

Consider each possibility in turn, thinking about whether the mood of the whole sonnet may be one of self-criticism or criticism of the young man.

---

defècts failings, imperfections
Whenas when
audit reckoning
advised respects careful thought
strangely pass walk by like a
  stranger

settled gravity weighty dignity
insconce shelter, defend
desert deservings
uprear raise

50

How heavy do I journey on the way,
When what I seek (my weary travel's end)
Doth teach that ease and that repose to say,
'Thus far the miles are measured from thy friend.'   4
The beast that bears me, tirèd with my woe,
Plods dully on, to bear that weight in me,
As if by some instìnct the wretch did know
His rider loved not speed being made from thee: 8
The bloody spur cannot provoke him on
That sometimes anger thrusts into his hide,
Which heavily he answers with a groan
More sharp to me than spurring to his side;   12
   For that same groan doth put this in my mind:
   My grief lies onward and my joy behind.

Sonnet 50 explores Shakespeare's sorrowful feelings as he travels on horseback away from his friend. Sonnet 51 will express his very different feelings as he makes the return journey.

Personification recurs throughout the sonnet. The horse carrying Shakespeare away from his friend is given human feelings of weariness and grief. Abstractions are also given human qualities: 'travel's end' can 'teach'; 'ease and that repose' can 'say'; 'anger' tries to spur the horse on.

The vocabulary and the rhythm of the sonnet suggest weariness and sorrow. Pick out all the words which imply tiredness or grief.

As you read this poem together with Sonnet 51, think about how far you agree with the suggestion that the horse may represent Shakespeare's conscience.

heavy slowly, sorrowfully
repose rest
beast horse
tirèd with wearied by, dressed in (attired)

weight sorrow
provoke urge
heavily sorrowfully
onward ahead
joy gladness, friend

51

Thus can my love excuse the slow offence
Of my dull bearer, when from thee I speed:
From where thou art, why should I haste me thence?
Till I return, of posting is no need.   4
O what excuse will my poor beast then find,
When swift extremity can seem but slow?
Then should I spur though mounted on the wind,
In wingèd speed no motion shall I know: 8
Then can no horse with my desire keep pace;
Therefore desire (of perfect'st love being made)
Shall neigh (no dull flesh) in his fiery race,
But love, for love, thus shall excuse my jade: 12
    Since from thee going he went wilful slow,
    Towards thee I'll run and give him leave to go.

Sonnet 51 begins by justifying the slow pace of the outward journey, travelling away from the friend. Lines 5–14 imagine the swift return journey. Desire is so strong that it results in 'wingèd speed', faster than the wind.

One interpretation of line 11 could be 'my horse will neigh with desire as he shakes off all feelings of tiredness, and races passionately homeward'. A different reading is, 'my desire will ignore all previously dull feelings as it thinks passionately of you'.

Try speaking Sonnets 50 and 51 as a single poem, to express their passionate and quick changes of thoughts and feelings.

---

slow offence fault of being slow
dull bearer tired horse
posting hurrying (post-haste)
swift extremity fastest speed
spur try to go faster
perfect'st the most perfect

fiery race passionate journey
jade horse
wilful stubbornly
give him leave to go allow him to
    gallop

So am I as the rich whose blessèd key
Can bring him to his sweet up-lockèd treasure,
The which he will not ev'ry hour survey,
For blunting the fine point of seldom pleasure.   4
Therefore are feasts so solemn and so rare,
Since, seldom coming, in the long year set,
Like stones of worth they thinly placèd are,
Or captain jewels in the carcanet.   8
So is the time that keeps you as my chest,
Or as the wardrobe which the robe doth hide,
To make some special instant special blest,
By new unfolding his imprisoned pride.   12
    Blessèd are you whose worthiness gives scope,
    Being had, to triumph, being lacked, to hope.

Sonnet 52 suggests that Shakespeare is still away from his friend, and is cheering himself up with the thought that infrequent meetings of lovers keeps their love strong. Such 'seldom pleasure' is like a rich man who only occasionally looks at his treasure, and so prevents his enjoyment from being blunted.

Similarly, occasional 'feasts' (feast-days, holidays) are spread thinly through the year, like large precious stones in a necklace. *King Henry IV, Part 1* (Act 1 Scene 2, lines 164–7) echoes the same thought:

If all the year were playing holidays,
To sport would be as tedious as to work;
But when they seldom come, they wished-for come,
And nothing pleaseth but rare accidents.

How far do you agree with the sonnet's claim that rare meetings between lovers are joyful, and that absence increases the anticipation of that joy?

So am I as I am like
For blunting for fear of blunting
solemn formal, ceremonious
stones of worth precious stones, jewels
captain chief

carcanet necklace
chest treasure-chest
his imprisoned pride its locked-up treasures
scope opportunity

53

What is your substance, whereof are you made,
That millions of strange shadows on you tend,
Since every one hath, every one, one shade,
And you, but one, can every shadow lend?   4
Describe Adonis, and the counterfeit
Is poorly imitated after you;
On Helen's cheek all art of beauty set,
And you in Grecian tires are painted new;   8
Speak of the spring and foison of the year:
The one doth shadow of your beauty show,
The other as your bounty doth appear,
And you in every blessèd shape we know.   12
    In all external grace you have some part,
    But you like none, none you, for constant heart.

Sonnet 53 uses the theory of the Greek philosopher, Plato (427–347 BC), that reality lies in essence ('substance') rather than in physical appearance or images ('shadow', 'shade', 'shape'). External appearances may change, but essence is unchanging ('constant'). The sonnet claims that the young man's essence contains the image of all beautiful things and persons.

Do you think the tone of the sonnet is sincere, or ironic (especially line 14)? To help your thinking, read it with these alternatives in mind:

Adonis in classical mythology, the perfect example of male beauty (but he coldly rejected love, and was killed whilst hunting).

counterfeit picture, description (or fake and false).

Helen Helen of Troy, the epitome of female beauty (but she was a model of inconstancy, unfaithful to her husband).

art of beauty all beauty's characteristics (or cosmetics, adornments which can conceal ugliness).

like (line 14) are similar to (or: care for).

---

substance essential nature
strange shadows images of others
tend attend (like servants)
every one hath ... shade each
  individual has their own unique
  appearance

lend supply, match every excellence
Grecian tires Greek dress or head-
  dress
foison rich harvest (autumn)
bounty rich harvest, generosity

O how much more doth beauty beauteous seem
By that sweet ornament which truth doth give!
The rose looks fair, but fairer we it deem
For that sweet odour which doth in it live.   4
The canker blooms have full as deep a dye
As the perfumèd tincture of the roses,
Hang on such thorns, and play as wantonly,
When summer's breath their maskèd buds discloses;   8
But, for their virtue only is their show,
They live unwooed, and unrespected fade,
Die to themselves. Sweet roses do not so,
Of their sweet deaths are sweetest odours made: 12
    And so of you, beauteous and lovely youth,
    When that shall vade, by verse distils your truth.

Sonnet 54 draws on themes found throughout Sonnets 1–126, including the young man's constancy, perfume, and the claim to immortality through poetry. It has the form of a careful, logical argument:

- Beauty is made more beautiful when it also possesses 'truth' (constancy, faithfulness).
- For example, a rose and a dog-rose look similarly beautiful. But dog-roses have no scent and die neglected, whereas roses have a scent which lives on, distilled into perfume.
- The young man has something extra, which distinguishes him from other beautiful people. His 'sweet ornament' is 'truth'.
- Shakespeare's verse will distil that truth, just as the scent of a rose can be distilled into perfume.

You may wish to turn to some sonnets which explore similar themes: Sonnets 53 and 116 (constancy), Sonnets 5, 6 and 99 (perfume), Sonnets 18, 55 and 60 (immortality through poetry).

---

sweet ornament additional quality
truth faithfulness, constancy
deem value, judge
canker blooms wild roses, dog-roses (having no scent)
dye colour

perfumèd tincture sweet smelling colour
wantonly freely, capriciously and carelessly
unwooed unloved, not plucked
sweetest odours perfumes
vade fade, perish

Nicholas Hilliard's miniature of an Elizabethan courtier captures the mood of melancholy love. The young man leans langorously on a tree, with his hand on his heart, caught by rosebush thorns, the symbol of unrequited passion. The rose, a symbol of love and beauty, occurs frequently throughout *The Sonnets*. Look out for the ways in which Shakespeare uses imagery of roses in other sonnets.

55

Not marble nor the gilded monuments
Of princes shall outlive this pow'rful rhyme,
But you shall shine more bright in these contènts
Than unswept stone, besmeared with sluttish time.   4
When wasteful war shall statues overturn,
And broils root out the work of masonry,
Nor Mars his sword nor war's quick fire shall burn
The living record of your memory.   8
'Gainst death and all oblivious enmity
Shall you pace forth; your praise shall still find room
Even in the eyes of all posterity
That wear this world out to the ending doom.   12
   So, till the Judgement that yourself arise,
   You live in this, and dwell in lovers' eyes.

Sonnet 55 celebrates poetry's power to ensure that someone is remembered after their death. It claims that poetry is more enduring than elaborate monuments, which are carelessly neglected ('unswept stone'). Poetry will survive the destruction of war, it will triumph over death and forgetfulness, and last until doomsday itself. The young man will live on in *The Sonnets* until judgement day, and as long as lovers can read.

A common feature of *The Sonnets* is paradox, or contradictory expressions. Here, the obvious paradox is the claim that paper (on which poetry is written) is stronger than stone, and can resist war, fire and death. But a greater paradox is present, in that it is Shakespeare himself who lives on in *The Sonnets*, and not the young man for whom they were written. He has disappeared into obscurity, and no one really knows who he was.

Identify all the ways in which poetry is described in lines 2, 3, 8, 10 and 14. Use them to decide whether or not you agree that poetry is more enduring than 'gilded monuments', outlasting stone memorials.

marble expensive tombstones
gilded decorated
sluttish dirty, neglected
broils battles
masonry stone buildings
Mars the Roman god of war

oblivious forgetful, unheedful
pace forth stride onward
posterity future generations
the ending doom judgement day,
  doomsday

The theme that poetry could outlast stone monuments was frequently explored by poets of the Renaissance. They drew on the idea expressed by classical authors, notably the Latin poets Horace and Ovid. For example, compare Sonnet 55 with the claim made by Ovid in his *Metamorphoses* that his verse would make him immortal:

> Now have I brought a work to end which neither Jove's fierce wrath
> Nor sword, nor fire, nor fretting age with all the force it hath
> Are able to abolish quite …
>   … And Time without all end
> (if poets by prophecy at the truth may aim)
> My life shall everlastingly be lengthened still by fame.

56

Sweet love, renew thy force, be it not said
Thy edge should blunter be than appetite,
Which but today by feeding is allayed,
Tomorrow sharp'ned in his former might.   4
So, love, be thou: although today thou fill
Thy hungry eyes even till they wink with fullness,
Tomorrow see again, and do not kill
The spirit of love with a perpetual dullness: 8
Let this sad int'rim like the ocean be
Which parts the shore, where two contracted new
Come daily to the banks, that when they see
Return of love, more blest may be the view;   12
   As call it winter, which being full of care,
   Makes summer's welcome, thrice more wished, more rare.

Sonnet 56 calls for love to be constantly renewed. It compares love to sexual or physical hunger which can be satisfied for a while, but which later
returns. This return of love is like the joy which lovers parted by the
ocean feel when their separation is ended, or like the welcome return of
summer after a long dreary winter.

Explaining the ambiguity in a poem can often kill the reader's enjoyment, but sometimes explanation can assist appreciation. Decide to what
extent you find the following explanation helpful to your appreciation of
Sonnet 56:

> The 'sad int'rim' (line 9) is pleasingly ambiguous. It might refer to a
> sorrowful period of absence, or to an estrangement, or to a growing
> indifference (apathy) on the part of the young man as the relationship
> cools. It might also mean refraining from lust.

---

edge keenness
appetite sexual desire, lust
allayed satisfied, relieved
wink with fullness doze after over-
  eating

int'rim estrangement, parting
two contracted new newly engaged
  lovers
As call it or call the interim

57

Being your slave, what should I do but tend
Upon the hours and times of your desire?
I have no precious time at all to spend,
Nor services to do till you require. 4
Nor dare I chide the world-without-end hour
Whilst I (my sovereign) watch the clock for you,
Nor think the bitterness of absence sour
When you have bid your servant once adieu. 8
Nor dare I question with my jealous thought
Where you may be, or your affairs suppose,
But like a sad slave stay and think of nought
Save where you are how happy you make those. 12
    So true a fool is love that in your will
    (Though you do any thing) he thinks no ill.

Throughout this sonnet, Shakespeare imagines himself as an abject slave, forced to wait endlessly and without reproach whilst the young man is absent, enjoying happiness with others. Use the following activities to help you explore Shakespeare's choice of words:

a Pick out all the words to do with time or service, for example, 'slave' and 'tend' in line 1.

b Read the sonnet aloud, emphasising all the 'negative' words ('no', 'nor', 'nought'). Think about how such words suggest lack of freedom.

c In line 13, 'will' could mean 'Will' (William Shakespeare) or 'desire'. If you wrote out the sonnet, would you write 'will' with a capital 'W' or a lower case 'w'?

d The tone of the sonnet has been described as 'devoted, but anxious submission' and as 'heavily sarcastic bitterness'. Do you prefer one of these views over the other? Give reasons for your choice.

---

tend attend, wait
precious time time of my own
chide rebuke, scold
world-without-end hour everlasting, so slowly moving time,
  endless waiting

once adieu farewell
suppose think or fantasise about
Save except

58

That god forbid, that made me first your slave,
I should in thought control your times of pleasure,
Or at your hand th'account of hours to crave,
Being your vassal bound to stay your leisure.   4
O let me suffer (being at your beck)
Th'imprisoned absence of your liberty,
And patience, tame to sufferance, bide each check,
Without accusing you of injury.   8
Be where you list, your charter is so strong
That you yourself may privilege your time
To what you will; to you it doth belong
Yourself to pardon of self-doing crime.   12
    I am to wait, though waiting so be hell,
    Not blame your pleasure, be it ill or well.

The slave imagery of Sonnet 57 is continued in Sonnet 58. Shakespeare imagines himself as the 'vassal' (dependant) of a feudal lord. He cannot demand to know how his master spends his time, but must patiently endure his absence without question. Like an all-powerful ruler, the young man has a 'charter' (legal right) to do as he wishes, and to be his own judge and jury.

a What is your attitude to the sonnet's portrayal of a lover as someone who feels like a devoted slave, willing to put up with anything, and never questioning any wrongdoing?

b Do you gain the impression that the young man is simply physically absent, or that he is now indifferent to Shakespeare and no longer returns his love?

c Does the sonnet strike you as expressing the genuine emotion of first-hand experience, or as a literary exercise, a poet exploring a theme without having actually lived through the experience?

That god Cupid, god of love
in thought even in imagination
crave wish for
vassal slave, feudal servant
stay your leisure wait upon your every wish

beck command
patience, tame ... check with patience, endure every rebuke
list desire, wish
privilege permit, authorise

59

If there be nothing new, but that which is
Hath been before, how are our brains beguiled,
Which, labouring for invention, bear amiss
The second burthen of a former child! 4
O that recòrd could with a backward look,
Even of five hundred courses of the sun,
Show me your image in some àntique book,
Since mind at first in character was done, 8
That I might see what the old world could say
To this composèd wonder of your frame:
Whether we are mended, or whe'er better they,
Or whether revolution be the same. 12
    O sure I am the wits of former days
    To subjects worse have given admiring praise.

Sonnet 59 recalls the proverb 'there is nothing new under the sun'. Lines 1–4 use the image of childbirth ('labouring', 'bear', 'burthen') to claim that poets, struggling to write something new, only awkwardly repeat their earlier creations. Lines 5–14 express the wish to know what earlier poets would have written about the young man's beauty.

Lines 11–12 probably focus on the quality of past and present poetry. They also offer three different views of human history, presenting alternative versions of human life on earth as:

- a story of progress ('we are mended')
- a story of decline from a previous Golden Age ('whe'er better they')
- history repeating itself ('whether revolution be the same').

Do you think that the couplet expresses a preference for one of these three viewpoints? Or could it be an ironic comment both on earlier writers and on the young man himself?

---

beguiled deceived
invention a new subject to write about
bear amiss wrongly create
second burthen re-birth
recòrd memory

courses of the sun years
character writing
composèd wonder written praise
revolution re-creation
wits poets
subjects worse inferior persons

60

Like as the waves make towards the pebbled shore,
So do our minutes hasten to their end,
Each changing place with that which goes before,
In sequent toil all forwards do contend.   4
Nativity, once in the main of light,
Crawls to maturity, wherewith being crowned,
Crookèd eclipses 'gainst his glory fight,
And Time that gave doth now his gift confound.   8
Time doth transfix the flourish set on youth,
And delves the parallels in beauty's brow,
Feeds on the rarities of nature's truth,
And nothing stands but for his scythe to mow.   12
    And yet to times in hope my verse shall stand,
    Praising thy worth, despite his cruel hand.

Sonnet 60 returns to the theme of the way in which poetry can transcend
the ravages of Time. Lines 1–12 stress the inevitability of age and death.
Like the unending movement of waves on a shingle beach, Time never
ceases its remorseless journey, bearing everything to death. The new-
born child will ultimately travel to the grave. Time will destroy the most
perfect and beautiful things in nature. Yet, in a longed-for future ('times
in hope') *The Sonnets* will defy Time's destructive power.

The imagery of the sonnet emphasises inevitability. The continual
motion of the waves echoes the never-ending passage of Time. The child,
born in an ocean ('main') of light, like the sun, is threatened with eclipse.
Youth's beauty is devastated by age. All things yield to Time's 'cruel
hand' as he mows down beauty with his scythe.

Try reading the sonnet aloud to emphasise how the pessimism of lines
1–12 is challenged by the couplet. Will you speak the 'And yet' of line 13
triumphantly, with quiet assurance, or in some other way?

---

sequent toil continually renewed
  efforts
contend strive
Nativity the new-born baby
Crookèd eclipses evil shadows
confound destroy

transfix the flourish destroy the
  bloom
delves the parallels digs wrinkles
rarities of nature's truth nature's
  most precious things

61

Is it thy will thy image should keep open
My heavy eyelids to the weary night?
Dost thou desire my slumbers should be broken,
While shadows like to thee do mock my sight?   4
Is it thy spirit that thou send'st from thee
So far from home into my deeds to pry,
To find out shames and idle hours in me,
The scope and tenure of thy jealousy?   8
O no, thy love, though much, is not so great;
It is my love that keeps mine eye awake,
Mine own true love that doth my rest defeat,
To play the watchman ever for thy sake.   12
    For thee watch I, whilst thou dost wake elsewhere,
    From me far off, with others all too near.

This sonnet describes the sleeplessness which results from feelings of jealousy (Sonnets 27 and 43 also explore the theme of sleeplessness). Lines 1–4 question why the young man's image torments Shakespeare, keeping him awake. Lines 5–8 imagine the young man's jealous spirit suspiciously searching Shakespeare's behaviour for shameful acts and time-wasting.

However, lines 9–14 reveal that it is Shakespeare's own jealousy which tortures him. Like all jealous people, he suspects that his beloved no longer loves him, and is unfaithful; others are 'all too near' the young man as he wakes.

Think about how accurately you feel the questioning tone of lines 1–8 expresses the anxiety caused by jealousy. Also consider the way in which the different meanings of 'wake' in line 13 reflect the worried suspicions of a jealous lover ('wake' means either awake, or revel, or grieve).

---

shadows images
spirit soul, attendant servant
pry suspiciously search
idle hours wasted time

scope and tenure target and meaning (or, range and fixation)
watchman night guard
watch keep awake, act as guard, look out for

62

Sin of self-love possesseth all mine eye,
And all my soul, and all my every part;
And for this sin there is no remedy,
It is so grounded inward in my heart.   4
Methinks no face so gracious is as mine,
No shape so true, no truth of such account,
And for myself mine own worth do define,
As I all other in all worths surmount.   8
But when my glass shows me myself indeed,
Beated and chopped with tanned antiquity,
Mine own self-love quite contrary I read;
Self so self-loving were iniquity.   12
    'Tis thee (my self) that for myself I praise,
    Painting my age with beauty of thy days.

Sonnet 62 reveals the gap between a false self-image and the reality of appearance. It ends with the poet asserting that his imagined beauty comes only from his thoughts of the young man.

Lines 1–8 express the delusions of self-love, as the poet thinks himself physically and morally superior to all others. But lines 9–12 expose the reality reflected in the mirror: an aged, lined face which makes 'self-loving' a sin. Only in the couplet is the truth acknowledged. Shakespeare imagines himself as the young man, ''Tis thee (my self)'. It is that thought which brings the illusion of beauty.

Does the sonnet 'ring true' to you? Does it feel like a poet writing about genuine experience, or does it seem to you to be a literary exercise?

---

self-love conceit, self-admiration
possesseth bewitches like madness
grounded rooted
define make clear
in all worths surmount surpass in value

indeed as I really am
Beated and chopped weather-beaten and lined
with tanned antiquity made leathery by old age
iniquity sin

63

Against my love shall be as I am now,
With Time's injurious hand crushed and o'erworn;
When hours have drained his blood and filled his brow
With lines and wrinkles; when his youthful morn   4
Hath travelled on to age's steepy night,
And all those beauties whereof now he's king
Are vanishing, or vanished out of sight,
Stealing away the treasure of his spring: 8
For such a time do I now fortify
Against confounding age's cruel knife,
That he shall never cut from memory
My sweet love's beauty, though my lover's life.   12
    His beauty shall in these black lines be seen,
    And they shall live, and he in them still green.

Shakespeare returns to the theme of verse ensuring that beauty lives on after death. Sonnet 63 anticipates the young man growing old, losing his beauty, and finally dying. In preparation for that time, Shakespeare claims that his sonnets ('these black lines') will keep the young man's memory alive and fresh. But Shakespeare was probably a comparatively young man when he wrote Sonnets 62 and 63. He was hardly likely to be as lined and wrinkled as the two sonnets claim.

The sonnet is rich in imagery, particularly metaphors of time: 'Time's injurious hand', 'youthful morn', and so on. Every line refers in some way to the passage of time. Consider each line in turn, and suggest how the 'time' words contribute to the mood of the sonnet.

Against in preparation for the time when
o'erworn worn out
steepy night decline into death

treasure of his spring perfection of his beauty
confounding destructive
knife scythe
green fresh and youthful

64

When I have seen by Time's fell hand defaced
The rich proud cost of outworn buried age;
When sometime lofty towers I see down rased,
And brass eternal slave to mortal rage;   4
When I have seen the hungry ocean gain
Advantage on the kingdom of the shore,
And the firm soil win of the wat'ry main,
Increasing store with loss, and loss with store;   8
When I have seen such interchange of state,
Or state itself confounded to decay,
Ruin hath taught me thus to ruminate:
That Time will come and take my love away.   12
    This thought is as a death, which cannot choose
    But weep to have that which it fears to lose.

In contrast to the preceding sonnet, the tone of Sonnet 64 seems entirely pessimistic. There is no hint that poetry can transcend death and keep alive the memory of beauty. The sonnet ends with the fearful thought that death will claim the love which now lives.

The sonnet may contain Shakespeare's reflections on what he saw as he travelled the country. For example, lines 3–4 could be a description of the abbey towers and church brasses that were destroyed in the Reformation (see also Sonnet 73). Lines 5–8 may, however, derive from Shakespeare's reading of Ovid's *Metamorphoses*, which similarly describes the sea and land gaining from each other, as the relentless ebb and flow of the tide changes the coastline. Sometimes the sea will gain ('store'), destroying cliffs. Sometimes the land gains, extending the shingle banks.

How far do you agree with the claim that 'line 8 is a perfect example of antithesis, exactly describing "the interchange of state" of sea and land'?

---

fell cruel
proud cost splendid and expensive buildings, boastful monuments
down rased levelled to the ground
brass eternal monumental brasses

mortal rage death's destructive fury
wat'ry main ocean
confounded destructively reduced
ruminate reflect

65

Since brass, nor stone, nor earth, nor boundless sea,
But sad mortality o'ersways their power,
How with this rage shall beauty hold a plea,
Whose action is no stronger than a flower?   4
O how shall summer's honey breath hold out
Against the wrackful siege of batt'ring days,
When rocks impregnable are not so stout,
Nor gates of steel so strong, but Time decays?   8
O fearful meditation! Where, alack,
Shall Time's best jewel from Time's chest lie hid?
Or what strong hand can hold his swift foot back,
Or who his spoil of beauty can forbid?   12
    O none, unless this miracle have might,
    That in black ink my love may still shine bright.

Sonnet 65 contrasts the fragility of beauty and human life with the destructive power of Time, which annihilates all things, however strong: brass, stone, earth, sea, rocks, steel. Time attacks summer itself, like an army besieging a town. This fearful thought provokes Shakespeare to ask how the young man ('Time's best jewel') can be preserved from the coffin ('Time's chest'). Lines 13–14 hope that *The Sonnets* can defy time and miraculously ensure that beauty lives on.

Time is again personified. Its destructive potential is described in vivid metaphors: 'sad mortality', 'this rage', and so on.

The sonnet poses a series of questions which provide the opportunity to explore different styles of reading. For example, quietly and rationally, as if considering an intellectual puzzle; or despairingly and anxiously, as if filled with pessimism and fear. How could the couplet be spoken to create a contrast with lines 1–12?

---

sad mortality inevitable death
o'ersways overrules
this rage death's fury
action life, power to resist
wrackful destructive

impregnable unconquerable
meditation thought
spoil plunder, destruction
might power

66

Tired with all these, for restful death I cry:
As to behold desert a beggar born,
And needy nothing trimmed in jollity,
And purest faith unhappily forsworn,   4
And gilded honour shamefully misplaced,
And maiden virtue rudely strumpeted,
And right perfection wrongfully disgraced,
And strength by limping sway disablèd,   8
And art made tongue-tied by authority,
And folly (doctor-like) controlling skill,
And simple truth miscalled simplicity,
And captive good attending captain ill: 12
    Tired with all these, from these would I be gone,
    Save that to die, I leave my love alone.

The form of Sonnet 66 is different from the familiar sonnet structure of
4 + 4 + 4 + 2. Lines 2–12 list the injustices which make Shakespeare long
for 'restful death'. He is only restrained by the thought that he would be
leaving his beloved. Each line gives examples of social evils, balancing
good with bad: worthy persons born into poverty (line 2); worthless persons dressed in fine clothes (line 3); religion or trust maliciously betrayed
(line 4), and so on.

Some readers try to root the list of evils in the social conditions of
Shakespeare's own times. Others say that similar corruptions exist today,
claiming, for example, that 'art' (education, the Arts) is still censored
('made tongue-tied by authority'), and that pompous ignorance ('folly,
doctor-like') crushes intelligence ('skill').

What do *you* think? Work through lines 2–12, a line at a time, asking
yourself if each line could describe a modern injustice. Also compare the
sonnet with Hamlet's 'To be or not to be' soliloquy.

As to behold for example to see
desert a deserving person, justice
gilded honour noble dignity
strumpeted made a prostitute

limping sway weak government
doctor-like like a pompous and
  ignorant teacher
simplicity stupidity

67

Ah wherefore with infection should he live,
And with his presence grace impiety,
That sin by him advantage should achieve,
And lace itself with his society? 4
Why should false painting imitate his cheek,
And steal dead seeming of his living hue?
Why should poor beauty indirectly seek
Roses of shadow, since his rose is true? 8
Why should he live, now Nature bankrout is,
Beggared of blood to blush through lively veins,
For she hath no exchequer now but his,
And proud of many, lives upon his gains? 12
    O him she stores, to show what wealth she had,
    In days long since, before these last so bad.

Sonnet 67 seems to follow the thought of the previous sonnet. It questions why the young man should live among such evils ('infection') listed in Sonnet 66, dignifying sin ('grace impiety') with his presence. Less attractive persons ('poor beauty') seek to imitate his true beauty, and Nature itself preserves ('stores') him to show what perfection was like in a past Golden Age ('days long since').

The sonnet uses imagery of cosmetics in lines 5–8 ('false painting'), and of finance in lines 9–13 ('bankrout', 'Beggared', 'exchequer', 'gains', 'wealth').

An alternative reading of the sonnet seems to question the perfection of the young man. He is flawed ('with infection'), and so gives dignity to sin ('grace impiety'), making it respectable and acceptable to society. Do you prefer one reading (unequivocal praise) over the other (qualified and critical praise), or do you feel that both are equally valid?

---

lace embellish, enrich
dead seeming lifeless imitation
hue complexion
Roses of shadow imitation beauty
rose beauty

bankrout bankrupt
Beggared of lacking
exchequer resources
proud of many desiring to produce
   many creatures

68

Thus is his cheek the map of days outworn,
When beauty lived and died as flowers do now,
Before these bastard signs of fair were borne,
Or durst inhabit on a living brow;   4
Before the golden tresses of the dead,
The right of sepulchres, were shorn away,
To live a second life on second head;
Ere beauty's dead fleece made another gay: 8
In him those holy àntique hours are seen,
Without all ornament, itself and true,
Making no summer of another's green,
Robbing no old to dress his beauty new;   12
    And him as for a map doth Nature store,
    To show false Art what beauty was of yore.

The sonnet contrasts natural beauty with artificial aids to beauty, such as cosmetics and wigs. It continues the argument of Sonnet 67 (notice it begins 'Thus'). The sonnet develops the theme of the Golden Age, a past time ('days outworn', 'holy àntique hours', 'of yore') when the young man's beauty exceeded all modern beauty.

Shakespeare's apparent dislike of cosmetics is evident: 'bastard signs of fair', 'ornament', 'false Art'. In lines 5–8, he scorns the practice of wearing wigs made from the hair of the dead, which was a fairly common practice in Elizabethan England. The young man needs no such false adornment. His natural appearance is the model ('map') for all beauty.

In the previous sonnet, Shakespeare described cosmetics as 'false painting'. Here, he increases his condemnation of artificial aids to beauty. Identify all the ways in which he describes such aids (see lines 3, 5, 8, 10, 11 and 14).

---

map perfect image
days outworn past times
bastard signs of fair false beauty, cosmetics
borne worn
durst dared

tresses locks of hair
The right of sepulchres which belonged to tombs
green youthful freshness
store preserve

69

Those parts of thee that the world's eye doth view
Want nothing that the thought of hearts can mend;
All tongues (the voice of souls) give thee that due,
Utt'ring bare truth, even so as foes commend.   4
Thy outward thus with outward praise is crowned,
But those same tongues that give thee so thine own,
In other accents do this praise confound
By seeing farther than the eye hath shown.   8
They look into the beauty of thy mind,
And that in guess they measure by thy deeds;
Then, churls, their thoughts (although their eyes were kind)
To thy fair flower add the rank smell of weeds: 12
    But why thy odour matcheth not thy show,
    The soil is this, that thou dost common grow.

Sonnet 69 claims that, although everyone praises the young man's outward appearance, those same admiring voices now question his inner qualities. His deeds do not match his external beauty, so his reputation ('odour') declines. Quite bluntly, it stinks ('the rank smell of weeds'). The final line reveals the reason for this blemished reputation: the young man has become vulgar ('common'), too much given to mixing freely with anyone, instead of keeping his distance from the friends of whom Shakespeare does not approve.

The contrast between external appearance and inner reality was one of Shakespeare's life-long preoccupations. It is evident in all his plays, for example in *Macbeth*: 'Look like the innocent flower, but be the serpent under it'. You will find other sonnets also concern themselves with outward beauty and inner corruption (see especially Sonnets 92, 93, 94 and 95).

Those parts of thee your outward appearance
Want lack
mend improve upon
even so ... commend as even enemies grudgingly praise

outward/outward appearance/public
confound confute, prove false
in guess by imagination
churls rude people
show outward appearance
soil reason

70

That thou are blamed shall not be thy defect,
For slander's mark was ever yet the fair;
The ornament of beauty is suspèct,
A crow that flies in heaven's sweetest air.   4
So thou be good, slander doth but approve
Thy worth the greater, being wooed of time,
For canker vice the sweetest buds doth love,
And thou present'st a pure unstainèd prime.   8
Thou hast passed by the ambush of young days,
Either not assailed, or victor being charged,
Yet this thy praise cannot be so thy praise
To tie up envy, evermore enlarged: 12
   If some suspèct of ill masked not thy show,
   Then thou alone kingdoms of hearts shouldst owe.

The slanderous accusations of Sonnet 69 are answered in Sonnet 70, which argues that beautiful people ('the fair') are always the target of malicious gossip. Such suspicious slander ('suspèct') accompanies beauty, like sinister crows in a clear sky. Indeed, this kind of slander proves the young man's innocence, because slander and suspicion inevitably seek out virtue to attack. The couplet asserts that, if it were not for the slander ('suspèct of ill') which clouds the young man's reputation ('masked not thy show'), everyone would love him.

Throughout the sonnet, slander is described in a variety of metaphors: as an arrow having a 'mark' (target); as 'suspèct', an 'ornament of beauty'; as a 'crow'; as a 'canker vice'; as an 'ambush' which assails or charges; as 'envy, evermore enlarged' (malice, always on the loose), and 'suspèct of ill'.

Consider each metaphor in turn. Suggest how appropriately it implies slander, the false and malicious gossip which discredits another person.

---

defect flaw (the 'soil' of Sonnet 69)
ornament accompaniment
So if
approve prove
wooed of time time's darling, universally loved

canker vice the cankerworm (see page 110)
unstainèd prime unblemished youth
cannot be so thy praise To is not such permanent praise as to
owe own

71

No longer mourn for me when I am dead
Than you shall hear the surly sullen bell
Give warning to the world that I am fled
From this vile world with vildest worms to dwell;   4
Nay, if you read this line, remember not
The hand that writ it, for I love you so
That I in your sweet thoughts would be forgot,
If thinking on me then should make you woe.   8
O if (I say) you look upon this verse,
When I (perhaps) compounded am with clay,
Do not so much as my poor name rehearse,
But let your love even with my life decay,   12
    Lest the wise world should look into your moan,
    And mock you with me after I am gone.

Sonnet 71 seems to be Shakespeare's simple reminder to his friend not to grieve for him after death, for fear of mockery (explained in Sonnet 72). Paradoxically, the sonnet is filled with reminders of the poet. Such reminders challenge the plea to be forgotten after death.

The Victorian poet Christina Rossetti was inspired to imitate the slow, sombre opening rhythm of Sonnet 71, but changed its theme to one of remembrance:

Remember me when I am gone away
Gone far away into the silent land;
When you can no more hold me by the hand,
Nor I half turn to go yet turning stay ...

One student described Sonnet 71 as 'emotional blackmail: it means the opposite of what it says, because it's really saying don't forget me after I'm dead'. To what extent do you agree with her interpretation?

---

surly sullen bell sombre funeral bell
vildest most vile
woe grieve
compounded mixed

rehearse repeat
Lest for fear that
moan sorrow
with me because of me

O lest the world should task you to recite
What merit lived in me that you should love,
After my death (dear love) forget me quite;
For you in me can nothing worthy prove,　　　4
Unless you would devise some virtuous lie
To do more for me than mine own desert,
And hang more praise upon deceasèd I
Than niggard truth would willingly impart:　　8
O lest your true love may seem false in this,
That you for love speak well of me untrue,
My name be buried where my body is,
And live no more to shame nor me nor you:　　12
　　For I am shamed by that which I bring forth,
　　And so should you, to love things nothing worth.

The sonnet tells the young man to 'forget me quite' if people ('the world') demand to know for what qualities he loved Shakespeare. Rather than invent 'some virtuous lie' praising the poet, it is better to forget him completely.

Shakespeare seems very self-deprecating, declaring himself 'nothing worthy' (line 4) and undeserving of praise (lines 5–8). He claims that he brings shame upon both the young man and himself because of 'that which I bring forth', which is 'nothing worth' (lines 13–14). Shakespeare may be thinking of *The Sonnets*, or his shame may come from being a playwright. People who worked in the theatre in the time of Queen Elizabeth I were considered to be of low social status.

Is Shakespeare speaking truthfully or ironically? Do you think it likely that he really felt as ashamed of his plays and poetry as he seems to be here? Consider what evidence there is in *The Sonnets* to justify your view.

---

lest for fear that
task command
recite tell
prove find, show
devise invent
desert deserving

hang more praise (like epitaphs on a tomb)
niggard miserly
untrue untruly, though I am unworthy

73

That time of year thou mayst in me behold
When yellow leaves, or none, or few, do hang
Upon those boughs which shake against the cold,
Bare ruined choirs, where late the sweet birds sang.   4
In me thou seest the twilight of such day
As after sunset fadeth in the west,
Which by and by black night doth take away,
Death's second self, that seals up all in rest.   8
In me thou seest the glowing of such fire
That on the ashes of his youth doth lie,
As the death-bed whereon it must expire,
Consumed with that which it was nourished by.   12
    This thou perceiv'st, which makes thy love more strong,
    To love that well which thou must leave ere long.

Sonnet 73 reflects on old age. In successive quatrains, it compares the poet's appearance as an old man to a tree losing its leaves as autumn changes to winter, to the setting sun, and to a dying fire choked by its own ashes. The sonnet's language is simple, but its imagery is richly ambiguous. In line 4, 'choirs' may be quires of paper, signifying written poetry; or the part of a cathedral where choristers ('sweet birds') sing; or the ruins of the monasteries destroyed in the Reformation. In line 8, 'seals' could refer to the sealing up of a coffin; to the sealing of a will by a dying person; or to the seeling (stitching) of a falcon's eyes, a common practice in Elizabethan falconry.

Do you think it is appropriate to interpret a sonnet in a way which Shakespeare could not have intended? For example, one student said of line 12: 'This is not just saying youthful love burns itself up, it is a metaphor for AIDS: love can kill'. What is your response to this interpretation?

---

behold see
late in earlier times, once

Consumed destroyed
perceiv'st see

74

But be contented when that fell arrest
Without all bail shall carry me away,
My life hath in this line some interest,
Which for memorial still with thee shall stay.   4
When thou reviewest this, thou dost review
The very part was consecrate to thee:
The earth can have but earth, which is his due;
My spirit is thine, the better part of me.   8
So then thou hast but lost the dregs of life,
The prey of worms, my body being dead,
The coward conquest of a wretch's knife,
Too base of thee to be rememberèd: 12
    The worth of that is that which it contains,
    And that is this, and this with thee remains.

In contrast to the pessimism of Sonnet 73, this sonnet offers consolation,
'But be contented'. After Shakespeare's death, his sonnets remain. They
contain his 'spirit' (soul, essence), and will keep him living on in the
young man's memory.

The sonnet sets body and spirit in opposition. The body constitutes
'the dregs of life', but the spirit, embodied in *The Sonnets*, is 'the better
part of me'. Line 7 echoes words from the Christian burial service, 'ashes
to ashes, dust to dust'. Line 11 has provoked very different interpretations, including Time's scythe, Shakespeare contemplating suicide, or
even the death of Christopher Marlowe (see page 93).

The couplet is full of pronouns: 'that', 'it', 'this', 'thee'. They refer either to the body or spirit, or to *The Sonnets*, or to the young man. Read the
couplet slowly, identifying the person or thing implied by each pronoun.

---

fell arrest cruel death
Without all bail with no possibility
 of release
this line these sonnets
interest right of possession
still always

was consecrate dedicated, which
 was sacred
due right
spirit soul, essence
dregs worthless remains
base unworthy

So are you to my thoughts as food to life,
Or as sweet seasoned showers are to the ground;
And for the peace of you I hold such strife
As 'twixt a miser and his wealth is found: 4
Now proud as an enjoyer, and anon
Doubting the filching age will steal his treasure;
Now counting best to be with you alone,
Then bettered that the world may see my pleasure: 8
Sometime all full with feasting on your sight,
And by and by clean starvèd for a look;
Possessing or pursuing no delight
Save what is had or must from you be took.   12
    Thus do I pine and surfeit day by day,
    Or gluttoning on all, or all away.

Sonnet 75 contains a wealth of balanced phrases or images: food/life, showers/ground, peace/strife, miser/wealth, enjoyer/steal, and so on. Similes are used to describe how the young man is seen in Shakespeare's loving thoughts. He is as necessary 'as food to life' or April showers to the earth. Shakespeare also says that he is like a miser experiencing mixed emotions about his wealth (the young man):

- enjoying him but fearing he may be stolen
- longing to be alone with him, but desiring to be seen with him
- enjoying the sight of him and afterwards longing to see him again, or longing desperately to receive a single glance
- receiving and desiring no other pleasure except the young man
- alternatively starved of love and feasting on it.

Match each description above with the appropriate lines in the sonnet. To what extent are the feelings described an accurate reflection of the typical emotions involved in passionate friendships?

sweet seasoned spring
for the peace of you hoping
  peacefully to enjoy your love
anon immediately
Doubting the filching age fearing
  these dishonest times

bettered thinking it better, made
  happier
pine starve
surfeit feast
Or gluttoning either overfeeding
all away nothing

Why is my verse so barren of new pride?
So far from variation or quick change?
Why with the time do I not glance aside
To new-found methods and to compounds strange?   4
Why write I still all one, ever the same,
And keep invention in a noted weed,
That every word doth almost tell my name,
Showing their birth, and where they did proceed?   8
O know, sweet love, I always write of you,
And you and love are still my argument;
So all my best is dressing old words new,
Spending again what is already spent: 12
    For as the sun is daily new and old,
    So is my love still telling what is told.

When reading *The Sonnets*, many students ask why Shakespeare chose to keep writing poetry in the same style. Sonnet 76 provides the answer. Shakespeare acknowledges that he hardly ever shifts from the pattern of three quatrains and a couplet, or from his theme of love. His 'invention' (topic or theme) and his 'method' (style) are always 'in a noted weed', namely the familiar 'dress' of the Shakespeare sonnet, which is so instantly recognisable that 'every word doth almost tell my name'.

Shakespeare's reply lies in the analogy in lines 13–14. Just as the sun rises and sets with inevitable regularity ('is daily new and old'), so Shakespeare will again and again write in sonnet form about his constant theme ('argument') of 'you and love'.

Think about the analogy which Shakespeare offers of the sun's rising and setting. Suggest how, within this regular pattern, it can be a source of never-ending fascination. It is the same, yet infinitely variable, never exhausted ('spent'), and never finally narrated or counted ('told').

---

barren empty
new pride fresh styles
variation or quick change variety
  or sudden shifts of style
with the time like today's fashion

compounds strange unfamiliar
  words and images
still always
argument topic, theme
all my best the best I can do

77

Thy glass will show thee how thy beauties wear,
Thy dial how thy precious minutes waste,
The vacant leaves thy mind's imprint will bear,
And of this book, this learning mayst thou taste: 4
The wrinkles which thy glass will truly show
Of mouthèd graves will give thee memory;
Thou by thy dial's shady stealth mayst know
Time's thievish progress to eternity;   8
Look what thy memory cannot contain
Commit to these waste blanks, and thou shalt find
Those children nursed, delivered from thy brain,
To take a new acquaintance of thy mind.   12
    These offices, so oft as thou wilt look,
    Shall profit thee, and much enrich thy book.

Sonnet 77 probably accompanied the gift of a blank notebook. It invites the young man to record his thoughts about age and death on the empty pages ('vacant leaves', 'waste blanks'). Such thoughts will be prompted by looking at his wrinkled face in a mirror, and watching the way in which a sundial slowly records the passage of time. Like children growing to maturity ('nursed'), the young man's writing will always be a fresh reminder of his thoughts.

The sonnet is in the tradition of *memento mori* (Latin for 'remember you will die'), which involves an object (like a skull) being given as a reminder of inevitable death. Today, such symbolic objects are rarely given, but Shakespeare's gift to his friend was not unusual for the times.

a Use the sonnet as the source of ideas for a cover design for a *memento mori* notebook.

b Explore the imaginative power of the imagery in line 8.

glass mirror	**mouthèd** gaping
wear fade	**shady stealth** creeping shadow
dial sundial	**Commit to** write on
vacant leaves blank pages	**waste blanks** blank pages
imprint shape, stamp	**delivered** born
this learning these lessons	**offices** duties

So oft have I invoked thee for my Muse,
And found such fair assistance in my verse,
As every alien pen hath got my use,
And under thee their poesy disperse.   4
Thine eyes, that taught the dumb on high to sing,
And heavy ignorance aloft to fly,
Have added feathers to the learnèd's wing
And given grace a double majesty.   8
Yet be most proud of that which I compile,
Whose influence is thine, and born of thee:
In others' works thou dost but mend the style,
And arts with thy sweet graces gracèd be;   12
   But thou art all my art, and dost advance
   As high as learning my rude ignorance.

Shakespeare expresses his fear that other poets are following his example and gaining favour and patronage from the young man. He acknowledges that the young man is his poetic inspiration ('Muse'), but seems to compare himself unfavourably to rival poets. Shakespeare describes himself as 'the dumb', 'heavy ignorance', 'rude ignorance', but describes the rival poets as 'the learnèd' and 'grace'.

The sonnet uses repetition of words and sounds to great effect. For example, the couplet echoes earlier mentions of 'high', 'ignorance' and 'art'. The vivid metaphors in lines 7 and 10 are from falconry (feathers were added to birds' wings to increase their flying ability), and from astrology, the 'influence' (of the stars).

An alternative interpretation is that Shakespeare is claiming that other poets are copying him, and that skill, rather than sincerity, characterises their poems. How convincing do you find this interpretation?

---

invoked called upon
Muse source of poetic inspiration
every alien pen other poets
under thee under your patronage
disperse circulate
on high melodiously

grace excellence
compile write, compose
influence power
mend improve
arts poetry, learning

Whilst I alone did call upon thy aid,
My verse alone had all thy gentle grace,
But now my gracious numbers are decayed,
And my sick Muse doth give another place.   4
I grant (sweet love) thy lovely argument
Deserves the travail of a worthier pen,
Yet what of thee thy poet doth invent
He robs thee of, and pays it thee again: 8
He lends thee virtue, and he stole that word
From thy behaviour; beauty doth he give,
And found it in thy cheek; he can afford
No praise to thee but what in thee doth live.   12
　　Then thank him not for that which he doth say,
　　Since what he owes thee, thou thyself dost pay.

Sonnet 79 expresses Shakespeare's concern about a rival poet. He sees his poetry decline, and his place in the young man's favour being taken by another, 'my sick Muse doth give another place'. He acknowledges the greater skill of the rival, 'a worthier pen', but bitterly complains that the rival is stealing, in verse, the virtue and beauty in the young man's behaviour and face.

The sonnet is very consciously 'poetic'. For example, the first two lines contain subtle internal rhymes, and lines 7–8 quietly reverse 'of thee'. Repetition is evident, particularly as Shakespeare's thought moves between the three characters involved: himself, the young man and the rival poet.

Try different ways of reading the sonnet to emphasise the 'triangle'. You could begin by speaking each mention of the rival as scornfully as possible (the first mention is in line 4).

---

aid inspiration, patronage
gracious numbers graceful verses
decayed lacking quality and
　patronage
another a rival poet

thy lovely argument the theme of
　your beauty
travail work
worthier pen better poet
afford offer

Christopher Marlowe: the rival poet? Sonnets 78–86 describe a rival poet who has stolen the young man's affection. Shakespeare regarded his rival as more educated, and a better poet than himself. The rival poet may have been Christopher Marlowe, who was, next to Shakespeare, the best known playwright in Elizabethan England. Marlowe was killed in mysterious circumstances in 1593. Some people even believe that Marlowe wrote *The Sonnets*.

This portrait from Corpus Christi College, Cambridge is reputed to be of Marlowe. Many other suggestions have been made as to the rival poet's identity. You can find some of them opposite Sonnet 86.

8o

O how I faint when I of you do write,
Knowing a better spirit doth use your name,
And in the praise thereof spends all his might,
To make me tongue-tied speaking of your fame. 4
But since your worth (wide as the ocean is)
The humble as the proudest sail doth bear,
My saucy bark (inferior far to his)
On your broad main doth wilfully appear. 8
Your shallowest help will hold me up afloat,
Whilst he upon your soundless deep doth ride,
Or (being wracked) I am a worthless boat,
He of tall building and of goodly pride. 12
    Then if he thrive and I be cast away,
    The worst was this: my love was my decay.

Shakespeare reveals more of his anxiety about the rival poet who may be displacing him in the young man's affection and patronage. Sonnet 80 acknowledges again his rival's skill, whose 'might' (poetic power) affects Shakespeare's own ability to write verse, making him 'tongue-tied'.

Using an image of sea and ships, Shakespeare seems to be cheering himself up. Like a 'saucy bark' (tiny boat), he can survive as well on the wide ocean of the young man's qualities and patronage as the 'proudest sail' (the rival poet). He needs only the 'shallowest help' to support him. This imagery may be a reference to the mighty Spanish Armada, which was defeated by smaller English ships.

Line 14 concludes that, even if Shakespeare ultimately loses out to his rival, the thought of lost love will comfort him. Taking the sonnet as a whole, do you think that Shakespeare's pessimism outweighs his effort to console himself?

better spirit superior poet
proudest sail most magnificent ship
saucy bark tiny, impudent boat
broad main wide ocean
wilfully disrespectfully

soundless deep bottomless sea
tall building huge size
goodly pride superb appearance
cast away abandoned

Or I shall live your epitaph to make,
Or you survive when I in earth am rotten,
From hence your memory death cannot take,
Although in me each part will be forgotten.   4
Your name from hence immortal life shall have,
Though I (once gone) to all the world must die;
The earth can yield me but a common grave,
When you intombèd in men's eyes shall lie: 8
Your monument shall be my gentle verse,
Which eyes not yet created shall o'er-read,
And tongues to be your being shall rehearse,
When all the breathers of this world are dead;   12
   You still shall live (such virtue hath my pen)
   Where breath most breathes, even in the mouths of men.

Sonnet 81 is strikingly ironic, but in a way that Shakespeare presumably did not intend. It promises the young man that *The Sonnets* will ensure that his memory lives on into future generations, whereas Shakespeare will be completely forgotten. The reverse is true! Today, Shakespeare enjoys world-wide fame, whilst even the identity of the young man is uncertain (see page 146).

In the first eight lines, the alternating rhythm and theme (whether you or I die first) established in lines 1 and 2 is repeated. The final six lines make a bold claim for the power of Shakespeare's verse ('such virtue hath my pen') to create an everlasting monument to the young man (see also Sonnet 18).

To reveal the unintended irony, read the sonnet aloud, changing the personal pronoun throughout (with the exception of 'my' in lines 9 and 13). For example, in line 1, 'I' becomes 'you', 'your' becomes 'my', and so on.

Or ... Or whether ... or
epitaph to make to write your funeral memorial
hence (line 5) these sonnets
intombèd remembered in a splendid tomb

tongues to be people yet unborn, future generations
being qualities, life
rehearse tell of
the breathers of this world people alive today
men humankind

82

I grant thou wert not married to my Muse,
And therefore mayst without attaint o'erlook
The dedicated words which writers use
Of their fair subject, blessing every book. 4
Thou art as fair in knowledge as in hue,
Finding thy worth a limit past my praise,
And therefore art inforced to seek anew
Some fresher stamp of the time-bettering days. 8
And do so, love; yet when they have devised
What strainèd touches rhetoric can lend,
Thou, truly fair, wert truly sympathised
In true plain words by thy true-telling friend; 12
   And their gross painting might be better used
   Where cheeks need blood; in thee it is abused.

Sonnet 82 appears to criticise both the young man and all rival poets. The first quatrain acknowledges that the young man is not solely tied to Shakespeare's verse, and may read others, but 'blessing every book' implies that he is not discriminating. He praises all poetry about himself, and is only too willing to extend his patronage to other poets who dedicate their work to him.

Lines 5–14 suggest that the young man finds Shakespeare's sonnets insufficient, and so seeks more fashionable poetry to praise him. But this other poetry, with its 'strainèd touches' (forced flourishes) is less true than Shakespeare's honest words (see page 187). The young man's beauty does not need such over-the-top flattery. Such 'gross painting' is more suited to less beautiful faces, 'Where cheeks need blood'.

All poets choose their words with great care, in order to heighten emphasis or to stress comparisons. Suggest ways in which the four variations on 'true' in lines 11–12 add to the quality of the sonnet.

(see page 187)

attaint dishonour
o'erlook read
dedicated devoted, praising
hue appearance
a limit past beyond
fresher stamp newer image

time-bettering days latest fashions
rhetoric fancy speaking
sympathised described with feeling
gross painting crude praises,
  thickly laid on flattery

I never saw that you did painting need,
And therefore to your fair no painting set;
I found (or thought I found) you did exceed
The barren tender of a poet's debt: 4
And therefore have I slept in your report,
That you yourself, being extant, well might show
How far a modern quill doth come too short,
Speaking of worth, what worth in you doth grow.   8
This silence for my sin you did impute,
Which shall be most my glory, being dumb,
For I impair not beauty, being mute,
When others would give life, and bring a tomb.   12
    There lives more life in one of your fair eyes
    Than both your poets can in praise devise.

The theme of Sonnet 82, that the young man's beauty needs no flattery or false 'painting', continues here. It seems that Shakespeare has not written any sonnets lately ('slept in your report'), because his friend's beauty speaks for itself. His silence has been seen as a sin (line 9), but Shakespeare himself sees it as a virtue, since when other poets seek to praise, they merely 'bring a tomb'. The couplet claims that neither Shakespeare nor any rival poet ('both your poets') can do justice to the young man's beauty.

a In line 3, Shakespeare slips in a qualification ('or thought I found') to the thought that the young man dislikes flattery. Do you think that this is a criticism of the young man?

b Is Shakespeare himself flattering the young man in this sonnet?

---

fair beauty
set applied
The barren tender ... debt such
  worthless offers to a patron
slept in your report written
  nothing about you

extant alive
modern quill ordinary poet
impute attribute, accuse
mute silent
a tomb lifeless poetry

84

Who is it that says most which can say more
Than this rich praise – that you alone are you,
In whose confine immurèd is the store
Which should example where your equal grew?   4
Lean penury within that pen doth dwell
That to his subject lends not some small glory,
But he that writes of you, if he can tell
That you are you, so dignifies his story: 8
Let him but copy what in you is writ,
Not making worse what nature made so clear,
And such a counterpart shall fame his wit,
Making his style admirèd every where.   12
    You to your beauteous blessings add a curse,
    Being fond on praise, which makes your praises worse.

Sonnet 84 begins by mocking those poets who overpraise the young man. They do not see that the richest praise would be to describe the young man just as he is ('you alone are you'). Only poor poets fail to praise, because they try too hard in their attempts to represent him. By contrast, any poets who can describe him accurately, and thereby praise him all the more, will become famous. However, the couplet seems to criticise the young man. His 'curse' is that he is foolishly fond of flattery, and so devalues the praise he gives to poets.

In line 3, the complex imagery of a richly filled walled garden ('immurèd' means walled-in) suggests that the young man contains within him many excellent qualities ('store').

Shakespeare advises poets to describe the young man just as he is, without using elaborate comparisons. Think about whether you find this advice at odds with Shakespeare's own practice in *The Sonnets*.

---

example … grew serve as the
  model for poems
Lean penury mean poverty
pen poet

counterpart poem, portrait, copy
fame his wit make his skill famous
fond on praise foolishly fond of
  flattery

85

My tongue-tied Muse in manners holds her still,
While comments of your praise, richly compiled,
Reserve their character with golden quill
And precious phrase by all the Muses filed. 4
I think good thoughts, whilst other write good words,
And like unlettered clerk still cry 'Amen'
To every hymn that able spirit affords
In polished form of well-refinèd pen. 8
Hearing you praised, I say, ''Tis so, 'tis true',
And to the most of praise add something more;
But that is in my thought, whose love to you
(Though words come hindmost) holds his rank before. 12
    Then others for the breath of words respect,
    Me for my dumb thoughts, speaking in effect.

The rival poet's superior skill is again acknowledged. Once more, Shakespeare describes himself as 'tongue-tied'. Like an illiterate churchman ('unlettered clerk'), he merely echoes approval ('Amen', ''Tis so, 'tis true') of more polished writing in praise of the young man. Yet his silent thoughts are filled only with love, far outstripping what can be said or written.

In the couplet, Shakespeare asks the young man to note ('respect') what others write, but to value him for his unspoken, sincere thoughts ('speaking in effect').

The sonnet's flowing rhythm is aided by much internal echoing of sounds of consonants: the 't' of 'tongue-tied', 'm' of 'Muse in manners', and so on. Read the sonnet aloud, stressing such repetitions and internal rhymes.

---

in manners ... still politely remains silent
comments of poems in
richly compiled fancifully written
Reserve their character record their praises

golden quill magnificent skill
filed polished
able spirit clever poet
come hindmost lag behind
holds his rank before (my loving thoughts) come first

Was it the proud full sail of his great verse,
Bound for the prize of all-too-precious you,
That did my ripe thoughts in my brain inhearse,
Making their tomb the womb wherein they grew?   4
Was it his spirit, by spirits taught to write
Above a mortal pitch, that struck me dead?
No, neither he, nor his compeers by night
Giving him aid, my verse astonishèd.   8
He, nor that affable familiar ghost
Which nightly gulls him with intelligence,
As victors, of my silence cannot boast;
I was not sick of any fear from thence;   12
    But when your countenance filled up his line,
    Then lacked I matter, that infeebled mine.

What was it about the rival poet which struck Shakespeare dumb ('my verse astonishèd')? Was it the rival's magnificent style ('proud full sail')? Was it his genius, aided by supernatural powers? Shakespeare concludes that none of these 'infeebled' his own verse. Rather, it was when the young man's 'countenance filled up his line', when the rival poet described his beauty and, in doing so, gained the favour which had previously been Shakespeare's.

Who were the 'spirits', 'compeers', and 'that affable familiar ghost'? You may find it helpful to keep at least three possibilities in mind as you read the sonnet:

Supernatural the ghostly guiding spirits which aid poets.

Contemporary associates the friends of the rival poet, whose quick-wittedness and literary interests aided his genius. One student suggested 'his drinking partners in an Elizabethan pub!'.

Authors of classical literature for example, Homer (see opposite).

Bound for the prize of seeking to capture
ripe thoughts blossoming sonnets (not yet written)
inhearse bury
Above a mortal pitch beyond human ability
compeers colleagues, allies
affable friendly
gulls deceives, crams
intelligence information
filled up his line became the subject-matter of his verse
matter subject-matter

George Chapman – the rival poet?

Thousands of words have been written about Sonnet 86, because it is seen as the crucial sonnet in determining the identity of the rival poet. George Chapman has often been suggested as Shakespeare's rival. He translated Homer's *Iliad* from Greek into English.

Those who support Chapman as the rival poet argue that, in Sonnet 86, the Greek authors whom he studied at night are his 'spirits' and 'compeers'. The 'affable familiar ghost' could refer to the poet Homer, since Chapman claimed to be inspired by him.

The case for Chapman is also made in terms of his elaborate style ('the proud full sail of his great verse') which soared like a falcon 'above a mortal pitch'. Chapman also wrote a poem entitled *'The Shadow of Night'*, which may be hinted at in lines 9–10.

Other contemporaries of Shakespeare who have been proposed as the rival poet include Christopher Marlowe (see page 93), Robert Greene (see Sonnet 112), Ben Jonson, George Peele, Michael Drayton, Samuel Daniel, Thomas Nashe, Thomas Lodge, Edmund Spenser, Richard Barnfield and Barnaby Rich. Even the Italian poet Dante, who died well over two hundred years before Shakespeare was born, has been suggested.

The truth is that no one can really know for sure, although many claim that their guess is right.

87

Farewell, thou art too dear for my possessing,
And like enough thou know'st thy estimate:
The charter of thy worth gives thee releasing;
My bonds in thee are all determinate.   4
For how do I hold thee but by thy granting,
And for that riches where is my deserving?
The cause of this fair gift in me is wanting,
And so my patent back again is swerving.   8
Thy self thou gav'st, thy own worth then not knowing,
Or me, to whom thou gav'st it, else mistaking;
So thy great gift, upon misprision growing,
Comes home again, on better judgement making: 12
    Thus have I had thee as a dream doth flatter,
    In sleep a king, but waking no such matter.

This sonnet implies that the young man has ended his relationship with Shakespeare. The imagery blends finance, emotion, law and social status. For example, in line 1, 'dear' could mean expensive, much loved, or of high status. Similarly, 'possessing' implies purchasing, legally owning, emotionally enjoying, and being socially appropriate.

Shakespeare acknowledges that he has enjoyed friendship only as a gift which can be withdrawn. Now, the young man's 'better judgement' has recognised his own high worth and Shakespeare's unworthiness. He has realised his mistake ('misprision'), and has withdrawn his 'great gift'. The couplet compares the friendship to a dream which grants king-like status. On waking to reality, however, the flattering illusion vanishes.

Sonnet 87 is unusual in having feminine endings, that is eleven syllables in a line rather than ten, with the last one unstressed. Turn to Sonnet 20 to read a poem in similar style.

---

like enough very probably
estimate value, price
The charter of thy worth your
  high status
releasing freedom
bonds claims

determinate ended
granting giving
wanting lacking
patent ... swerving right of
  ownership returns to you

88

When thou shalt be disposed to set me light,
And place my merit in the eye of scorn,
Upon thy side against myself I'll fight,
And prove thee virtuous, though thou art forsworn: 4
With mine own weakness being best acquainted,
Upon thy part I can set down a story
Of faults concealed wherein I am attainted,
That thou in losing me shall win much glory;   8
And I by this will be a gainer too,
For, bending all my loving thoughts on thee,
The injuries that to myself I do,
Doing thee vantage, double vantage me.   12
    Such is my love, to thee I so belong,
    That for thy right myself will bear all wrong.

There are echoes of Sonnet 49 in this sonnet. Shakespeare foresees a time when the young man will despise him and expose him to contempt ('the eye of scorn'). When that time comes, Shakespeare will support the rejection, and even confess further faults. Anything which benefits the young man serves Shakespeare's love for him.

Consider to what extent the following students' views reflect your own responses to the sonnet:

a 'This is self-sacrifice gone mad. He's saying he's happy to do himself injury by perjuring his own reputation because those lies will help raise the young man's esteem. It just doesn't make sense.'

b 'This is the sonnet of the true lover, because "That for thy right myself will bear all wrong" expresses the most devoted love.'

c 'This is mainly a literary exercise, not expressing deep feeling. It's more about using antithesis as many times as possible.'

---

disposed to set me light inclined to despise me
the eye of scorn contempt
forsworn false
Upon thy part in your support
attainted tainted, disgraced

bending turning, twisting
vantage advantage
right truth, justice
bear all wrong accept injustice, speak falsely

89

Say that thou didst forsake me for some fault,
And I will comment upon that offence;
Speak of my lameness, and I straight will halt,
Against thy reasons making no defence.　　　　　　4
Thou canst not (love) disgrace me half so ill,
To set a form upon desirèd change,
As I'll myself disgrace, knowing thy will:
I will acquaintance strangle and look strange,　　　8
Be absent from thy walks, and in my tongue
Thy sweet belovèd name no more shall dwell,
Lest I (too much profane) should do it wrong,
And haply of our old acquaintance tell.　　　　　12
　　For thee, against myself I'll vow debate,
　　For I must ne'er love him whom thou dost hate.

The theme of Sonnet 88 continues here. Once again, Shakespeare says that, if the young man rejects him, he will not protest. He will add more reasons for that rejection, avoid all further contact, and never speak of their past friendship. If the young man hates him, he will make war on himself ('against myself I'll vow debate'). He will disgrace himself far more than the young man could.

The sonnet may contain implicit criticism of the young man. Line 6 suggests that he may be concerned with what other people will think. He wants to 'set a form upon' (make look good) what he wants to happen (the 'desirèd change'), namely ending the friendship.

Some people interpret line 3 as an indication that Shakespeare was lame (see also Sonnet 37). Others interpret 'lameness' as 'writing poor poetry'. Does one interpretation seem more probable to you than the other? Give reasons for your decision.

---

forsake abandon
comment upon tell more about
halt limp, stop arguing
reasons arguments
will desire

acquaintance strangle kill our
　friendship
look strange be distant
profane blasphemous, an outsider
haply by chance
debate war, conflict

90

Then hate me when thou wilt, if ever, now,
Now while the world is bent my deeds to cross,
Join with the spite of Fortune, make me bow,
And do not drop in for an after-loss.   4
Ah do not, when my heart hath scaped this sorrow,
Come in the rearward of a conquered woe;
Give not a windy night a rainy morrow,
To linger out a purposed overthrow.   8
If thou wilt leave me, do not leave me last,
When other petty griefs have done their spite,
But in the onset come; so shall I taste
At first the very worst of Fortune's might;   12
    And other strains of woe, which now seem woe,
    Compared with loss of thee, will not seem so.

Sonnet 90 urges the young man to break the relationship swiftly and immediately. It hints that Shakespeare is already assailed by misfortune ('bent my deeds to cross'), but wants first to experience the worst that can happen, the loss of the young man. This loss makes all other kinds of injury ('strains of woe') seem trivial.

The image of an attacking army pervades the sonnet. Shakespeare begs the young man to be in the vanguard ('the onset') of the assaults, and not to delay his intended rejection ('linger out a purposed overthrow').

To help you understand how the sonnet achieves its effects, identify:

a all the words which suggest a military assault.

b all the words suggesting urgency, to emphasise the theme of 'reject me now – not later' (for example, 'Then', 'now', and so on).

c all the imperatives (commands) which create a pleading tone (for example, 'hate me', 'Join with', and so on).

---

wilt will, desire
bent resolved, determined
my deeds to cross to defeat me
drop in for an after-loss attack
  after the main battle
scaped escaped

the rearward of final assault upon
linger out prolong
purposed overthrow intended
  defeat
onset first wave of attack
strains kinds

Some glory in their birth, some in their skill,
Some in their wealth, some in their body's force,
Some in their garments, though new-fangled ill,
Some in their hawks and hounds, some in their horse;   4
And every humour hath his adjunct pleasure,
Wherein it finds a joy above the rest;
But these particulars are not my measure:
All these I better in one general best.   8
Thy love is better than high birth to me,
Richer than wealth, prouder than garments' cost,
Of more delight than hawks or horses be;
And having thee, of all men's pride I boast: 12
   Wretched in this alone, that thou mayst take
   All this away, and me most wretched make.

The sonnet lists the things which some people feel boastfully proud about ('glory in'): breeding, intelligence, wealth, strength, clothes and hunting prowess. Every 'humour' or temperament has its accompanying passion ('adjunct pleasure'). But Shakespeare claims that these particular passions are surpassed by his love for his friend. The couplet reveals a familiar anxiety, that the only thing which can cause unhappiness is if the young man ceases to love him.

Repetition is a technique used by poets to increase the intensity and aesthetic appeal of their verse (see page 191). Pick out the different ways in which repetition is used in Sonnet 91. For example, 'Some' in the first quatrain, the echoes of the contents of the first quatrain in the third quatrain, and so on.

---

birth hereditary status
skill intelligence, dexterity
force strength
new-fangled ill trendy but vulgar
horse horses, hunting

my measure what I judge by, my yardstick
I better in one general best I surpass with something far superior

---

But do thy worst to steal thyself away,
For term of life thou art assurèd mine,
And life no longer than thy love will stay,
For it depends upon that love of thine.   4
Then need I not to fear the worst of wrongs,
When in the least of them my life hath end;
I see a better state to me belongs
Than that which on thy humour doth depend.   8
Thou canst not vex me with inconstant mind,
Since that my life on thy revolt doth lie.
O what a happy title do I find,
Happy to have thy love, happy to die!   12
　　But what's so blessèd-fair that fears no blot?
　　Thou mayst be false, and yet I know it not.

Sonnet 92 continues the thought of the preceding sonnet, as the 'But' in
line 1 picks up on lines 13–14 of Sonnet 91. It draws comfort from the
thought that Shakespeare's love is life-long, and his life will end when the
young man ceases to love him. He will not fear losing the young man ('the
worst of wrongs'), because the slightest hint that love is over ('the least of
them') will cause death. Lines 11–12 celebrate constant happiness: in life
with the young man's love, and in death when that love is withdrawn.

However, the couplet casts a shadow over the apparent optimism of
lines 1–12. The young man may be unfaithful, and Shakespeare may be
unaware of it.

Compare lines 11–12 with lines 13–14. Describe the difference in
mood between them. Do you think that they are equally sincere, truly reflecting Shakespeare's feelings?

---

steal thyself away leave me
　(echoing Sonnet 91)
term of life my lifetime
assurèd certainly
least of them smallest show of your
　lack of love

humour whim, temperament
vex annoy, charge
inconstant mind changing moods
revolt unfaithfulness
title claim to ownership
blot flaw

93

So shall I live, supposing thou art true,
Like a deceivèd husband; so love's face
May still seem love to me, though altered new;
Thy looks with me, thy heart in other place: 4
For there can live no hatred in thine eye,
Therefore in that I cannot know thy change.
In many's looks, the false heart's history
Is writ in moods and frowns and wrinkles strange,   8
But heaven in thy creation did decree
That in thy face sweet love should ever dwell;
What e'er thy thoughts or thy heart's workings be,
Thy looks should nothing thence but sweetness tell.   12
    How like Eve's apple doth thy beauty grow,
    If thy sweet virtue answer not thy show!

The anxious thought in the couplet of Sonnet 92 is taken up here. If the young man is false, Shakespeare will be like a deceived husband. To all outward appearances, the young man is unchanged, but he may only 'seem' so (line 3).

The sonnet explores one of Shakespeare's favourite themes, namely that appearances can be deceptive. Some people's faces show their inner character, whereas others conceal corruption behind a pleasant appearance (see pages 183 and 195). The young man's appearance is always outwardly loving, even if his heart is 'in other place'.

The couplet suggests that this false appearance of beauty and love is 'like Eve's apple'. In the story of Adam and Eve in the Bible, Eve was tempted by a serpent (the devil) to eat the beautiful, but corrupting, fruit from the tree of knowledge of good and evil.

Use the sonnet to explore the idea that character is reflected in a person's face.

---

supposing imagining, falsely believing
altered new loving someone else
in other place with another lover
many's looks many people's faces
in thy creation when you were born

decree ordain, command
heart's workings true feelings
thence on your face
answer not does not match
show outward appearance

94

They that have pow'r to hurt, and will do none,
That do not do the thing they most do show,
Who, moving others, are themselves as stone,
Unmovèd, cold, and to temptation slow –   4
They rightly do inherit heaven's graces,
And husband nature's riches from expense;
They are the lords and owners of their faces,
Others but stewards of their excellence.   8
The summer's flow'r is to the summer sweet,
Though to itself it only live and die,
But if that flow'r with base infection meet,
The basest weed outbraves his dignity: 12
    For sweetest things turn sourest by their deeds;
    Lilies that fester smell far worse than weeds.

Sonnet 94 seems to praise powerful people who refrain from doing harm, and who do not show their emotions, but present an 'Unmovèd, cold' face to the world. Like a flower blossoming unseen, their self-possession preserves their virtues and their qualities. But if they become corrupt, their corruption is more vile than that of even the worst of people ('Lilies that fester smell far worse than weeds').

The sonnet may be deeply ironic, criticising those who control their emotions so firmly. The irony comes from several sources: partly from the ambiguous tone of the language; partly from the immediately preceding sonnet's expression of anxiety about the mismatch of outward appearance and true feelings; and partly from Sonnets 1–17, which urged that 'nature's riches' should be spent, not husbanded, contradicting the sentiment of line 6.

Do you think that the sonnet approves or disapproves of people who show no emotion, those who are 'lords and owners of their faces'?

---

heaven's graces divine gifts
husband carefully protect
expense waste
stewards managers
excellence finer passions, noble qualities

base infection corruption
outbraves surpasses, is more splendid than
his dignity its beauty
Lilies flowers symbolising purity

95

How sweet and lovely dost thou make the shame
Which, like a canker in the fragrant rose,
Doth spot the beauty of thy budding name!
O in what sweets dost thou thy sins inclose!   4
That tongue that tells the story of thy days
(Making lascivious comments on thy sport)
Cannot dispraise, but in a kind of praise,
Naming thy name, blesses an ill report.   8
O what a mansion have those vices got
Which for their habitation chose out thee,
Where beauty's veil doth cover every blot,
And all things turns to fair that eyes can see!   12
    Take heed (dear heart) of this large privilege:
    The hardest knife ill used doth lose his edge.

The generalised thoughts of Sonnet 94 are made personal in this sonnet, which addresses the young man directly, asserting that his vices are concealed beneath a beautiful appearance. Rumours of his sexual exploits are given a kind of prestige or dignity merely by using his name: 'Naming thy name, blesses an ill report'. But the couplet warns that sexual licence leads to loss of 'edge' (reputation, sexual appetite, vitality).

The imagery of lines 1–12 includes: 'canker' (the cankerworm, which destroys the beauty of the rose from within, but shows only a tiny spot on the outside), 'sweets' (perfume), 'mansion' (body or dwelling) and 'veil'. The couplet introduces a different metaphor, that of beauty which, like a roughly treated knife, can be destroyed by bad use.

Think about whether the couplet to Sonnet 94 could be substituted for lines 13–14 of Sonnet 95. Do you feel that such a substitution would maintain or destroy the integrity of this sonnet?

---

spot blemish, corrupt
budding name youthful or growing
  reputation
Making lascivious comments
  spreading suggestive rumours

sport sexual activities
blot flaw, blemish
large privilege wide freedom
ill used roughly treated

96

Some say thy fault is youth, some wantonness,
Some say thy grace is youth and gentle sport;
Both grace and faults are loved of more and less:
Thou mak'st faults graces that to thee resort.   4
As on the finger of a thronèd queen
The basest jewel will be well esteemed,
So are those errors that in thee are seen
To truths translated, and for true things deemed.   8
How many lambs might the stern wolf betray,
If like a lamb he could his looks translate!
How many gazers mightst thou lead away,
If thou wouldst use the strength of all thy state!   12
But do not so; I love thee in such sort,
As thou being mine, mine is thy good report.

Contrasting views of the young man are presented here. He is both praised and criticised for his youthfulness and behaviour. Vivid images illustrate the claim that he turns vices into virtues: 'Thou mak'st faults graces that to thee resort'. Lines 5–8 claim that, just as a cheap jewel on a queen's finger becomes highly esteemed, so the young man gives dignity to 'errors' or faults. Like a wolf in sheep's clothing, he could, if he wished, seduce ('lead away') many.

The couplet is identical to the couplet of Sonnet 36 (don't misbehave, because my love for you means that my reputation depends on yours). Some people believe that Shakespeare forgot to write a couplet for Sonnet 96, so the printer chose one for him from an earlier sonnet.

Decide how well you think the couplet 'fits' the sonnet. If you had to replace it with another, which would you choose? Alternatively, write your own couplet to conclude the sonnet.

---

wantonness sexual misbehaviour
grace virtue
gentle sport gentlemanly pastimes
of more and less by everybody
  (persons of high and low status)
translated transformed

If like a lamb … translate if he
  could disguise himself as a lamb
gazers admirers
wouldst wished to
state power, personality, glamour

97

How like a winter hath my absence been
From thee, the pleasure of the fleeting year!
What freezings have I felt, what dark days seen!
What old December's bareness every where!   4
And yet this time removed was summer's time,
The teeming autumn big with rich increase,
Bearing the wanton burthen of the prime,
Like widowed wombs after their lords' decease: 8
Yet this abundant issue seem'd to me
But hope of orphans, and unfathered fruit,
For summer and his pleasures wait on thee,
And thou away, the very birds are mute;   12
    Or if they sing, 'tis with so dull a cheer
    That leaves look pale, dreading the winter's near.

Sonnet 97 reflects on a period of separation or estrangement. The central images are of the seasons and of childbirth. Separation from the young man is like winter: cold, dark and bare. But the time of absence was actually 'summer's time, The teeming autumn', full of the rich harvest of what was planted in the spring.

The harvest itself seemed fatherless, 'Like widowed wombs after their lords' decease'. The image is of life springing forth after the father (spring) is dead. Since the young man is the source of all happiness, without him, everything seems like winter.

One way of thinking about the sonnet is to see it as an example of the 'pathetic fallacy', where nature mirrors human moods. Human unhappiness is reflected in the bareness of winter. When lovers are separated, birds do not sing, leaves look pale, and so on. Look out for further examples of the pathetic fallacy as you read other sonnets.

---

fleeting quickly passing
time removed absence
teeming fruitful, fertile
big with rich increase pregnant
  with fruitfulness

Bearing the wanton ... the prime
  delivering spring's uncontrolled
  fertility
abundant issue rich harvest
mute silent

98

From you have I been absent in the spring,
When proud-pied April (dressed in all his trim)
Hath put a spirit of youth in every thing,
That heavy Saturn laughed and leapt with him.   4
Yet nor the lays of birds, nor the sweet smell
Of different flowers in odour and in hue,
Could make me any summer's story tell,
Or from their proud lap pluck them where they grew: 8
Nor did I wonder at the lily's white,
Nor praise the deep vermilion in the rose;
They were but sweet, but figures of delight,
Drawn after you, you pattern of all those.   12
 Yet seemed it winter still, and, you away,
 As with your shadow I with these did play.

The theme of the way in which absence causes sadness continues, but this
sonnet seems to be referring to an earlier period of separation. In spite of
the glories of April, which made even sad Saturn happy (the planet
Saturn was believed to cause melancholy), nothing could cheer
Shakespeare. He recognised the sweetness of spring flowers, but they
seemed merely images ('figures') of delight, unable to equal the ideal of
excellence ('pattern') embodied in the young man. Everything seemed
like winter. The flowers, like the remembered image of the young man,
were no real substitute for his presence.

 Both April and the planet Saturn are personified in lines 1–4, but is
the sonnet an example of the pathetic fallacy? Turn back to Sonnet 97 to
remind yourself of how the pathetic fallacy works in poetry. Then decide
whether Sonnet 98 is similar in kind, or whether it shows nature in a
mood quite different from Shakespeare's own feelings.

proud-pied brilliantly multi-
 coloured
trim fine clothes
heavy sad
lays songs
hue colour

summer's story happy tale
proud lap lovely meadows (earth)
vermilion red or scarlet
figures images
you away in your absence

99

The forward violet thus did I chide:
'Sweet thief, whence didst thou steal thy sweet that smells,
If not from my love's breath? The purple pride
Which on thy soft cheek for complexion dwells   4
In my love's veins thou hast too grossly dyed.'
The lily I condemnèd for thy hand,
And buds of marjoram had stol'n thy hair;
The roses fearfully on thorns did stand,   8
One blushing shame, another white despair;
A third, nor red nor white, had stol'n of both,
And to his robb'ry had annexed thy breath,
But for his theft in pride of all his growth   12
A vengeful canker eat him up to death.
    More flowers I noted, yet I none could see
    But sweet or colour it had stol'n from thee.

Sonnet 99 develops a thought from the preceding sonnet about the way in which nature copies the young man's beauty. It accuses the violet of stealing the young man's fragrance and colour, the lily of taking its whiteness from his hand, and marjoram of copying the colour of his hair. Even roses steal their colour and odour from him (and their theft will be punished by destruction by a cankerworm).

This sonnet is the only fifteen-line poem in the sequence; the first quatrain contains five lines instead of four. No one knows whether the sonnet is a draft which Shakespeare forgot to revise, or whether he always intended it to have fifteen lines.

Some critics think that the tone of the sonnet is insincere and artificial. They argue that Shakespeare was copying another poet's sonnet, and became bored with the exercise. How far do you agree with this theory?

forward early, precocious
chide rebuke
sweet that smells odour, fragrance
complexion colour
too grossly very obviously

condemnèd for thy hand accused of stealing the whiteness of your hand
annexed added (also stolen)
canker cankerworm (see page 110)
But except

100

Where art thou, Muse, that thou forget'st so long
To speak of that which gives thee all thy might?
Spend'st thou thy fury on some worthless song,
Dark'ning thy pow'r to lend base subjects light?   4
Return, forgetful Muse, and straight redeem
In gentle numbers time so idly spent;
Sing to the ear that doth thy lays esteem,
And gives thy pen both skill and argument.   8
Rise, resty Muse, my love's sweet face survey,
If Time have any wrinkle graven there;
If any, be a satire to decay,
And make Time's spoils despisèd every where.   12
    Give my love fame faster than Time wastes life;
    So thou prevent'st his scythe and crookèd knife.

Sonnet 100 begins a sequence in which Shakespeare rebukes his 'Muse' or poetic inspiration for neglecting to write about the young man. The sonnet has been interpreted as Shakespeare's criticism of his own playwriting ('worthless song', 'base subjects'). Lines 7–8 suggest that the young man values *The Sonnets*, as well as being their inspiration and topic ('argument').

The sonnet returns to the theme of Time's destructive power. If the young man shows signs of ageing ('any wrinkle'), then *The Sonnets* should be 'a satire to decay', satirical verses which condemn Time, mocking its ravages. In this way, they will give the young man fame, and defeat Time ('prevent'st his scythe and crookèd knife').

The questions of the first four lines give way to a series of orders ('Return', 'straight redeem', and so on). Identify other words in lines 5–14 which give the sonnet its sense of urgency.

Spend'st thou why do you waste
fury poetic energy
base inferior
straight redeem immediately
  compensate for

gentle numbers noble verses,
  excellent poetry
lays songs
resty lazy, sleepy
graven etched, cut
spoils ravages, plunder

O truant Muse, what shall be thy amends
For thy neglect of truth in beauty dyed?
Both truth and beauty on my love depends;
So dost thou too, and therein dignified.   4
Make answer, Muse, wilt thou not haply say,
'Truth needs no colour with his colour fixed,
Beauty no pencil, beauty's truth to lay;
But best is best, if never intermixed'?   8
Because he needs no praise, wilt thou be dumb?
Excuse not silence so, for't lies in thee
To make him much outlive a gilded tomb,
And to be praised of ages yet to be.   12
     Then do thy office, Muse; I teach thee how
     To make him seem long hence as he shows now.

As in Sonnet 100, Shakespeare questions why his 'Muse' has neglected to praise the young man, who is the perfect example of moral honesty and loveliness blended, 'truth in beauty dyed'. The sonnet imagines the Muse using imagery from painting (lines 5–8) to reply that such perfection needs no addition and no adulteration with words ('intermixed'). However, lines 9–14 remind poetry of its duty ('office') to make the young man's present qualities live 'to be praised of ages yet to be', when readers 'long hence' will be able to see him as he is at this moment.

The sonnet's use of 'truth' and 'beauty' shows the way in which a poet can create many interpretations from seemingly simple words. Think about how Shakespeare uses the two words in lines 1–8, and brainstorm possible meanings, using a thesaurus or dictionary to help you. Also consider the way in which the words are linked together: 'truth in beauty', 'truth and beauty', 'beauty's truth'.

---

truant absent
amends excuse, recompense
my love (the young man)
dignified given dignity
haply perhaps

colour disguise, painting, essence, nature
pencil painter's brush
lay apply, paint
gilded artificially decorated

102

My love is strength'ned, though more weak in seeming;
I love not less, though less the show appear:
That love is merchandised whose rich esteeming
The owner's tongue doth publish every where.   4
Our love was new, and then but in the spring,
When I was wont to greet it with my lays,
As Philomel in summer's front doth sing,
And stops his pipe in growth of riper days: 8
Not that the summer is less pleasant now
Than when her mournful hymns did hush the night,
But that wild music burthens every bough,
And sweets grown common lose their dear delight.   12
　　Therefore like her, I sometime hold my tongue,
　　Because I would not dull you with my song.

Shakespeare claims that his love has increased, although the fact that he
has written less poetry may seem to suggest that it has cooled. Love is
cheapened by those who constantly proclaim it ('publish every where'),
and familiarity only breeds contempt ('sweets grown common').

The sonnet uses simile and metaphor, comparisons in which words
stand for something different from their literal meaning. Like the
nightingale ('Philomel') which sings at night in the spring but falls silent
in summer when other birds sing loudly, so Shakespeare wrote sonnets in
the early days of love, but wrote less frequently as love matured, and as
rival poets clamoured for the young man's attention. He has no wish to
bore the young man with too many verses (lines 13–14). But even though
he is silent, his love is as strong as ever.

Work through lines 5–14 suggesting how Shakespeare uses comparisons with the seasons and with bird-song to explain why he has written
fewer sonnets of late. Use the paragraph above to help you.

---

seeming appearance
the show outward signs
merchandised bought and sold,
　cheapened
esteeming value　　　　　　，
wont accustomed

lays songs
summer's front early summer
his pipe singing
riper days late summer
burthens weighs down, echoes from
dull bore

Alack, what poverty my Muse brings forth,
That, having such a scope to show her pride,
The argument all bare is of more worth
Than when it hath my added praise beside.   4
O blame me not if I no more can write!
Look in your glass, and there appears a face
That overgoes my blunt invention quite,
Dulling my lines, and doing me disgrace.   8
Were it not sinful then, striving to mend,
To mar the subject that before was well?
For to no other pass my verses tend
Than of your graces and your gifts to tell;   12
    And more, much more than in my verse can sit,
    Your own glass shows you, when you look in it.

Shakespeare adds yet another reason to explain why he has found it so difficult to write. The young man, 'The argument all bare', is more beautiful in himself than in any poetic description Shakespeare can write. Any portrayal becomes merely 'blunt invention' (unimaginative poetry), putting the poet to shame. Poetry will 'mar' (spoil) what is already perfect, that is, the reflection the young man sees in the mirror.

Some readers think that line 14 is implicitly critical of the young man. It suggests that he is self-regarding, admiring his own reflection in a mirror which shows only his outward appearance.

Sonnets 100, 101, 102 and 103 are all on the same theme, that Shakespeare has stopped writing poetry, or is finding great difficulty in doing so. If you had to place them in sequence (for a poetry reading, for instance), would you present them in their existing order, or would you rearrange them? Give reasons for your decision.

poverty poor poetry   **overgoes** surpasses, defeats
a scope an opportunity   **Dulling** making dull
pride splendid creativity   **pass** end, purpose
glass mirror   **tend** aim

104

To me, fair friend, you never can be old,
For as you were when first your eye I eyed,
Such seems your beauty still. Three winters cold
Have from the forests shook three summers' pride, 4
Three beauteous springs to yellow autumn turned
In process of the seasons have I seen,
Three April perfumes in three hot Junes burned,
Since first I saw you fresh which yet are green. 8
Ah yet doth beauty, like a dial hand,
Steal from his figure, and no pace perceived;
So your sweet hue, which methinks still doth stand,
Hath motion, and mine eye may be deceived; 12
    For fear of which, hear this, thou age unbred:
    Ere you were born was beauty's summer dead.

Sonnet 104 is often quoted in arguments about whether or not *The Sonnets* are autobiographical (see pages 3–4). Some people claim that Shakespeare is reflecting here on three years of friendship with the young man. Those who do not agree with the autobiography theory point out that other poets before Shakespeare also wrote sonnets about love which has lasted for three years.

Lines 9–12 fear that, although the young man's beauty still seems the same after three years, this perception may be mistaken. The image is of a sundial or the hand of a clock. It does not appear to move, 'no pace perceived', and yet it inevitably records the passage of time. As you read lines 9–10, keep in mind the following possibilities:

dial hand hand of clock, shadow on a sundial, Time as a person.
Steal from creep like the hand of a clock, or like a thief.
figure number on a clock face, essence of beauty, the young man.

---

your eye I eyed I saw you
pride splendid foliage
April ... burned fading of spring
  flowers (or incense made from
  April's flowers)
green young
pace movement

hue appearance
age unbred times unborn, future
  ages
Ere before
beauty's summer the height of
  beauty (the young man)

105

Let not my love be called idolatry,
Nor my belovèd as an idol show,
Since all alike my songs and praises be
To one, of one, still such, and ever so.   4
Kind is my love today, tomorrow kind,
Still constant in a wondrous excellence;
Therefore my verse, to constancy confined,
One thing expressing, leaves out difference.   8
'Fair, kind, and true' is all my argument,
'Fair, kind, and true', varying to other words,
And in this change is my invention spent,
Three themes in one, which wondrous scope affords.   12
   'Fair', 'kind', and 'true' have often lived alone,
   Which three till now never kept seat in one.

Like Sonnet 76, this sonnet defends the practice of always writing on the same subject, the young man. Asking not to be thought of as idolatrous (worshipping false gods), Shakespeare uses religious language to claim that he always writes to, and about, the same person, 'To one, of one', and in the same style, 'still such, and ever so'. This constancy mirrors the constancy of the young man, in that it is always fair, kind and true.

The sonnet's repetitions are like a litany or repeated prayer. They echo the Christian doctrine of the Trinity (three in one) which Shakespeare heard every Sunday in church: 'Glory be to the father and to the Son, and to the Holy Ghost. As it was in the beginning, is now and ever shall be, world without end.' The following possibilities suggest the 'wondrous scope' (amazing range) of meanings:

fair beauty, just, pure, honourable.
kind generous, gentle, loving, natural, benevolent.
true natural integrity, honesty, constancy, true beauty.

---

show appear
Since because
songs and praises sonnets
Still constant always unvarying
difference variety, conflicts, changes
argument theme

varying to other words expressed in different words
invention spent poetic imagination used
kept seat in one lived together in one person

106

When in the chronicle of wasted time
I see descriptions of the fairest wights,
And beauty making beautiful old rhyme
In praise of ladies dead and lovely knights,   4
Then in the blazon of sweet beauty's best,
Of hand, of foot, of lip, of eye, of brow,
I see their àntique pen would have expressed
Even such a beauty as you master now.   8
So all their praises are but prophecies
Of this our time, all you prefiguring,
And for they looked but with divining eyes
They had not skill enough your worth to sing: 12
    For we, which now behold these present days,
    Have eyes to wonder, but lack tongues to praise.

Shakespeare remembers the older literature he has read, such as
Chaucer. The sonnet's archaic language recalls these ancient tales of
chivalry and romance ('wights', 'knights', 'blazon').

These same tales praised the beauty of long-ago knights and ladies,
predicting ('prefiguring') the beauty of the young man. However, the
older poets lacked the skill to praise him sufficiently, because they never
actually saw him. In contrast, Shakespeare and his contemporaries can
see the young man, but lack the poetic skill ('tongues') to do justice to his
beauty.

a Keep turning the phrase 'the chronicle of wasted time' over in your
   mind. What thoughts, images and feelings does it call up?

b Do you gain the impression that the sonnet is claiming 'modern'
   (Elizabethan) poetry is inferior or superior to 'ancient' poetry? Or do
   you feel it avoids this kind of comparison?

---

the chronicle ancient stories
wights persons
lovely good-looking, much loved
blazon coat of arms, list of
  admirable qualities

master possess, control
prefiguring predicting,
  foreshadowing
And for unless
divining prophetic

107

Not mine own fears, nor the prophetic soul
Of the wide world, dreaming on things to come,
Can yet the lease of my true love control,
Supposed as forfeit to a confined doom.   4
The mortal moon hath her eclipse endured,
And the sad augurs mock their own presàge,
Incertainties now crown themselves assured,
And peace proclaims olives of endless age.   8
Now with the drops of this most balmy time
My love looks fresh, and Death to me subscribes,
Since spite of him I'll live in this poor rhyme,
While he insults o'er dull and speechless tribes.   12
    And thou in this shalt find thy monument,
    When tyrants' crests and tombs of brass are spent.

This sonnet returns to the theme that poetry will triumph over death, thus ensuring that the young man lives on. Lines 1–4 reject the fears or prophecies that Shakespeare's love will end. Lines 10–14 claim victory over death, which can only defeat people who have no poetry, the 'dull and speechless tribes'. Verse will endure long after elaborate and boastful memorials have decayed into ruin ('crests and tombs of brass are spent').

Many attempts have been made to set a date when the sonnet was written. Lines 5–9 probably refer to actual historical events, but as you can see opposite, there are many theories, but little agreement!

Use the information opposite to make up your own mind which date you think is the most likely. You may want to do some historical research into a particular event, and write your own argument supporting that date. On the other hand, you may prefer to ignore all the historical interpretations and enjoy the sonnet simply for its poetic qualities.

---

the prophetic soul … world the world's fearful expectation
dreaming on prophesying
lease duration
control determine, end

Supposed as … doom believed to be subject to the penalty of inescapable fate
balmy healthy
subscribes submits
insults triumphs
crests battle-helmets, coats of arms

Line 5

The mortal moon hath her eclipse endured.

1603 Queen Elizabeth has died (she was often compared to Diana, virgin goddess of the moon).

1601 Queen Elizabeth has survived the rebellion by the Earl of Essex.

1599–1600 Queen Elizabeth has survived a major illness (this was a rumour of the time, but in fact she suffered no such illness).

1595–6 Queen Elizabeth has survived her Grand Climacteric (her sixty-third year, thought by astrologers to be a year of ill-omen).

1595 The moon has undergone a total eclipse.

1593–4 Queen Elizabeth has survived an assassination attempt by her personal physician, Dr Lopez.

1588 The Spanish Armada has been defeated (the ships of the Armada fought in a crescent, moon-like formation).

Line 6

And the sad augurs mock their own presàge.

Who were the melancholy prophets of doom who laughed at their earlier fearful predictions of disaster? As you can imagine, claims have been made for all the people who had gloomy and fearful expectations of each event listed above.

Lines 7–8

Incertainties now crown themselves assured,
And peace proclaims olives of endless age.

When was this particular time when uncertainties were resolved and a time of everlasting peace seemed in promise? (The olive branch is a traditional symbol of peace.) Once again, you can imagine that such hope followed every one of the events listed above, when the feared disaster did not occur.

Consider some of the arguments for 1603. Many people in England were fearful about what would happen after Queen Elizabeth's death, as no clear successor existed, and civil war was predicted. But the accession to the throne by King James I in 1603 was relatively smooth. Public proclamations were made that a time of enduring peace had arrived, 'this most balmy (healthy) time'. The new king released the Earl of Southampton from imprisonment in the Tower of London. If Southampton really was the young man of *The Sonnets* (see page 146), it may be his release that is referred to in lines 9–10.

108

What's in the brain that ink may character
Which hath not figured to thee my true spirit?
What's new to speak, what now to register,
That may express my love, or thy dear merit?   4
Nothing, sweet boy; but yet, like prayers divine,
I must each day say o'er the very same,
Counting no old thing old, thou mine, I thine,
Even as when first I hallowèd thy fair name.   8
So that eternal love in love's fresh case
Weighs not the dust and injury of age,
Nor gives to necessary wrinkles place,
But makes antiquity for aye his page,   12
    Finding the first conceit of love there bred,
    Where time and outward form would show it dead.

Shakespeare questions what there is new to say that has not already been
said in *The Sonnets*. He answers 'Nothing', and claims that, like prayers
which are repeated daily, *The Sonnets* must express their familiar theme,
'thou mine, I thine'. Like a prayer, this constant repetition ignores age.
Love makes time its servant; it always finds, even in the young man's
changed appearance or in the old form of words, the everlasting truth of
the very first verses written about the young man's beauty.

a One student said, 'Line 7, "thou mine, I thine", is what *The Sonnets*
   are all about, and what real love is about'. To what extent do you agree
   with her?

b Every poet tries to ensure that his or her language expresses as fully as
   possible the theme of the poem. Try to work out the ways in which
   lines 5–8 express the theme of 'prayers divine', frequently repeated
   prayers. For example, in line 8, there is an echo of the Lord's Prayer.

character write
register write down
hallowèd made holy, blessed
fresh case youthful appearance, new
 poetry
Weighs not ignores

necessary wrinkles old age
for aye eternally
page young servant
conceit thought, poetic expression
outward form appearance

O never say that I was false of heart,
Though absence seemed my flame to qualify;
As easy might I from my self depart
As from my soul, which in thy breast doth lie: 4
That is my home of love. If I have ranged,
Like him that travels I return again,
Just to the time, not with the time exchanged,
So that myself bring water for my stain.   8
Never believe, though in my nature reigned
All frailties that besiege all kinds of blood,
That it could so preposterously be stained
To leave for nothing all thy sum of good;   12
   For nothing this wide universe I call,
   Save thou, my rose; in it thou art my all.

Sonnet 109 begins a sequence of 'absence' sonnets. It seems that Shakespeare has been on his travels, and is now writing to claim his love is unchanged by absence. He counts the universe as nothing in comparison to the young man ('my rose'), who means everything to him.

But the sonnet can be read differently. Instead of a physical absence, caused by travel, it could refer to Shakespeare's affections straying elsewhere. His passionate nature, filled with 'All frailties', may have caused him to love another (or others). Alternatively, the sonnet may be a kind of apology for not having written any poetry recently.

Read the sonnet first with the notion of physical travel in mind, and then again thinking about the idea of unfaithfulness. Try a third reading considering it as an apology for the lack of sonnets written recently. Do all three readings feel equally valid to you?

---

false of heart unfaithful
flame love, poetic power
qualify reduce
ranged strayed, travelled
Just to the time punctual, faithful

water for my stain tears (or
  sonnets) to wash away my offence
preposterously absurdly
sum of good total excellence
Save except

Alas 'tis true, I have gone here and there,
And made myself a motley to the view,
Gored mine own thoughts, sold cheap what is most dear,
Made old offences of affections new.   4
Most true it is that I have looked on truth
Askance and strangely; but, by all above,
These blenches gave my heart another youth,
And worse essays proved thee my best of love.   8
Now all is done, have what shall have no end:
Mine appetite I never more will grind
On newer proof, to try an older friend,
A god in love, to whom I am confined.   12
      Then give me welcome, next my heaven the best,
      Even to thy pure and most most loving breast.

This sonnet is often interpreted as Shakespeare commenting critically on his own experience as an actor. He has toured or appeared on many stages ('gone here and there'), and played the fool in front of audiences ('to the view') like a clown ('motley'). But a different reading sees Shakespeare owning up to the emotional betrayal of his friend. He has become a public laughing stock, dishonouring himself through new love affairs ('affections new').

In lines 5–14, Shakespeare claims that he has learned from bitter experience ('worse essays') that the young man is his 'best of love', to whom he dedicates himself for ever ('have what shall have no end'). He will no longer test that love by trying out different loves ('newer proof'). The young man is his god, second only to heaven.

Imagine that a student asks you, 'Are both interpretations in the first paragraph above equally valid?'. Make your reply.

Gored wounded
Askance sideways, disdainfully
strangely as a stranger
by all above by all that is holy
blenches sidelong glances, blemishes

another youth renewed freshness
appetite passions
grind sharpen
newer proof different lovers
confined solely committed

O for my sake do you with Fortune chide,
The guilty goddess of my harmful deeds,
That did not better for my life provide
Than public means which public manners breeds.   4
Thence comes it that my name receives a brand,
And almost thence my nature is subdued
To what it works in, like the dyer's hand.
Pity me then, and wish I were renewed,   8
Whilst like a willing patient I will drink
Potions of eisel 'gainst my strong infection;
No bitterness that I will bitter think,
Nor double penance to correct correction.   12
    Pity me then, dear friend, and I assure ye
    Even that your pity is enough to cure me.

Shakespeare regrets that he is forced to earn a living as an actor and play-wright. Such 'public means' (having to appear on stage) breeds 'public manners' (vulgar and superficial behaviour). Actors in Shakespeare's time had low social status, so his reputation has become dishonoured: 'my name receives a brand'. The coarseness of his work affects his very nature, just as a dyer's hand becomes stained by the dyes he uses daily.

In lines 9–14, Shakespeare begs for a cure for his 'stain', no matter how bitter. He will voluntarily suffer any 'double penance' (double dose of self-inflicted punishment to wash away sin), but his friend's pity will be enough to cure him.

There is a memorable image of the 'dyer's hand' in lines 6–7. Think of examples which you think validate (or contradict) this image. Does a person's nature change to become more and more like the nature of his or her work? Do 'dirty' jobs produce 'dirty' people?

Fortune goddess of human destiny
chide rebuke
name receives a brand reputation
  is dishonoured

subdued To reduced to, over-
  powered by
renewed cured
Potions of eisel draughts of vinegar
  (medicine to cure the plague)

112

Your love and pity doth th'impression fill
Which vulgar scandal stamped upon my brow,
For what care I who calls me well or ill,
So you o'er-green my bad, my good allow?   4
You are my all the world, and I must strive
To know my shames and praises from your tongue;
None else to me, nor I to none alive,
That my steeled sense or changes right or wrong.   8
In so profound abysm I throw all care
Of others' voices, that my adder's sense
To critic and to flatterer stoppèd are.
Mark how with my neglect I do dispense: 12
    You are so strongly in my purpose bred
    That all the world besides methinks th'are dead.

Sonnet 112 begins with an image from the previous sonnet of criminals who were branded on the forehead, leaving a hollow scar ('impression'). Shakespeare claims that his public disgrace (working as an actor) is compensated for by the young man's love and pity. He takes no notice of whatever critics or flatterers say. Like the adder, he is deaf to such voices.

In line 4, 'o'er-green' is usually interpreted as 'make fresh' or 'cover over', like replacing a worn turf in a lawn with a new one. Alternatively, it may refer to Robert Greene, who launched a violent personal attack on Shakespeare in 1592 (see page 204).

Don't worry if you have difficulty with lines 7–8 – many people do. Their general sense may be 'Neither I nor anyone else can change my fixed nature, whether for good or bad'. Perhaps they were a first draft, and Shakespeare intended, but forgot, to rewrite them. Try your own hand at rewriting the lines to fit the sense of the sonnet.

---

allow approve
steeled fixed
profound abysm bottomless gulf
adder's sense deaf ears (adders were thought to be deaf)
stoppèd are refuse to listen

with my neglect I do dispense I excuse my refusal to listen to the voices
in my purpose bred living in my thoughts

112

Y Our loue and pittie doth th'impreffion fill,
  Which vulgar fcandall ftampt vpon my brow,
For what care I who calles me well or ill,
So you ore-greene my bad,my good alow?
You are my All the world,and I muft ftriue,
To know my fhames and praifes from your tounge,
None elfe to me,nor I to none aliue,
That my fteel'd fence or changes right or wrong,
In fo profound *Abifme* I throw all care
Of others voyces,that my Adders fence,
To cryttick and to flatterer ftopped are:
Marke how with my negle&t I doe difpence.
      You are fo ftrongly in my purpofe bred,
      That all the world befides me thinkes y'are dead.

Sonnet 112 first appeared in print when *The Sonnets* were published in 1609.
No one knows if Shakespeare gave his permission for the publication. Compare
this original version with the modern typeset version opposite.
Pick out as many differences as you can.

The Sonnets have been republished many times since 1609, and every
editor makes adjustments to the original version. Imagine that you have
been invited to edit Sonnet 112 for inclusion in a new edition of *The Sonnets*
for school and college students. Use the 1609 original to write out
your own version of the sonnet.

113

Since I left you, mine eye is in my mind,
And that which governs me to go about
Doth part his function, and is partly blind,
Seems seeing, but effectually is out;   4
For it no form delivers to the heart
Of bird, of flow'r, or shape which it doth latch;
Of his quick objects hath the mind no part;
Nor his own vision holds what it doth catch: 8
For if it see the rud'st or gentlest sight,
The most sweet favour or deformèd'st creature,
The mountain, or the sea, the day, or night,
The crow, or dove, it shapes them to your feature.   12
    Incapable of more, replete with you,
    My most true mind thus maketh mine eye untrue.

Sonnet 113 is an extended exploration of the thought that 'lovers see only their beloved', or 'we see what we want to see'. The sonnet plays on the difference between eye and mind, the difference between what registers on the eye and what is 'seen' in the mind. Absence so fills Shakespeare's mind with the young man's image that it distorts his vision. Whatever his eye sees, his mind changes it to resemble the young man's features.

The eye/mind contrast is reflected in the antitheses of lines 9–12: 'rud'st'/'gentlest', 'sweet favour'/'deformèd'st', 'mountain'/'sea', and so on.

Pick out in each line the words which mean (or refer to) the eye. For example, 'eye' in line 1, all of line 2, 'his' in line 3, and so on. Only lines 10 and 11 do not contain such a reference.

---

that which governs ... about (my eye)
Doth part his function divides its purpose
effectually is out in effect sees wrongly
form shape

latch catch sight of
his quick objects the eye's fleetingly seen things
rud'st most vulgar
Incapable of more unable to do more
replete filled only

114

Or whether doth my mind being crowned with you
Drink up the monarch's plague, this flattery?
Or whether shall I say mine eye saith true,
And that your love taught it this alcumy,   4
To make of monsters, and things indigest,
Such cherubins as your sweet self resemble,
Creating every bad a perfect best
As fast as objects to his beams assemble?   8
O 'tis the first, 'tis flatt'ry in my seeing,
And my great mind most kingly drinks it up;
Mine eye well knows what with his gust is greeing,
And to his palate doth prepare the cup.   12
    If it be poisoned, 'tis the lesser sin
    That mine eye loves it and doth first begin.

This sonnet follows on directly from Sonnet 113. It questions what
makes everything seen by the eye or mind resemble the young man. Is it
flattery, like the insincere praise which deceives kings, or 'alcumy'
(alchemy), the false magic which tries to turn base matter into gold? The
sonnet concludes that flattery is the answer.

A 'kingly' image runs through the sonnet. The eye is like a king's
winetaster, mixing wine (shaping everything to resemble the young man)
which the king (the mind) will enjoy. The couplet may contain an implicit criticism of the young man, suggesting that the sight of him may be
poisoned like the wine. But the eye cannot take full blame ('the lesser sin')
for being the first to see what it loves before the mind does.

In deciding that the eye flatters the mind with pleasing pictures, the
sonnet uses imagery of monarchy, alchemy and drink. Suggest one or two
reasons why each image is appropriate to the theme of flattery.

the monarch's plague the
  occupational hazard of the king
saith speaks
indigest shapeless
cherubins angels

his beams assemble (the belief
  that beams from the eye created
  images)
gust taste
greeing agreeing
palate taste

115

Those lines that I before have writ do lie,
Even those that said I could not love you dearer;
Yet then my judgement knew no reason why
My most full flame should afterwards burn clearer.   4
But reckoning Time, whose millioned accidents
Creep in 'twixt vows, and change decrees of kings,
Tan sacred beauty, blunt the sharp'st intents,
Divert strong minds to th'course of alt'ring things –   8
Alas, why, fearing of Time's tyranny,
Might I not then say 'Now I love you best',
When I was certain o'er incertainty,
Crowning the present, doubting of the rest?   12
    Love is a babe: then might I not say so,
    To give full growth to that which still doth grow.

Shakespeare reflects on the way in which love, which seems perfect and complete, can continue to grow. He claims that earlier sonnets have lied in saying that his love could not be greater.

Lines 5–12 acknowledge that Time alters all things: vows of love, judgements of kings, beautiful faces, the firmest intentions. Why then, ask lines 9–12, is it unwise to say, 'Now I love you best'? After all, only the present is certain, and the future can only be doubtful and uncertain. The couplet gives a confident reply: like a baby, love will grow, and it is the knowledge of this which stopped the poet from saying 'Now I love you best'.

a Time is personified twice in lines 5–9. Try to conjure up a picture in your mind for both images.

b *The Sonnets* are primarily love poems. Do you consider lines 5–8 to be a statement of fact, cynical or ironic judgements, or … ?

---

dearer more intensely
full flame extreme passion
reckoning calculating, always
  counting up
millioned accidents millions of
  chance happenings

decrees judgements, laws
Tan spoils, make leathery
th'course of alt'ring things
  inevitable change
Crowning glorifying

116

Let me not to the marriage of true minds
Admit impediments; love is not love
Which alters when it alteration finds,
Or bends with the remover to remove.   4
O no, it is an ever-fixèd mark
That looks on tempests and is never shaken;
It is the star to every wand'ring bark,
Whose worth's unknown, although his heighth be taken.   8
Love's not Time's fool, though rosy lips and cheeks
Within his bending sickle's compass come;
Love alters not with his brief hours and weeks,
But bears it out even to the edge of doom.   12
    If this be error and upon me proved,
    I never writ, nor no man ever loved.

Sonnet 116 may be the most famous and most quoted of all Shakespeare's sonnets. Lines 1–2 echo the Christian marriage service, 'If any of you know any cause, or just impediment ...'. The sonnet defines perfect love through negatives: love does not change when other things change, it is not the fool of Time. It also defines such love in images and direct statements: love is as stable as a lighthouse or the North Star, lasting unchanged until doomsday.

The sonnet's confident assertion of the enduring power of love, which triumphs over time and death, gives it great appeal. So, too, does its use of words to conjure up intriguing possibilities which enrich meaning. For example, in line 4, 'the remover' may be an unfaithful person, someone who leaves a loving relationship, or Time itself, which removes all things.

a Learn Sonnet 116 by heart. Which are your favourite lines?

b Design a cover for an edition of *The Sonnets*, based on Sonnet 116.

---

impediments obstacles
bends ... remove changes when the
  other person's love changes
mark lighthouse, beacon
star the North Star
bark ship

heighth be taken position is
  measured
bending sickle's compass curved
  scythe's sweep
bears it out endures
edge of doom doomsday

Accuse me thus: that I have scanted all
Wherein I should your great deserts repay,
Forgot upon your dearest love to call,
Whereto all bonds do tie me day by day;   4
That I have frequent been with unknown minds,
And given to time your own dear-purchased right;
That I have hoisted sail to all the winds
Which should transport me farthest from your sight.   8
Book both my wilfulness and errors down,
And on just proof surmise accumulate;
Bring me within the level of your frown,
But shoot not at me in your wakened hate;   12
    Since my appeal says I did strive to prove
    The constancy and virtue of your love.

Shakespeare asks to be accused of neglecting his obligations to the young man, and of wasting his time with far less worthy persons. He wants to add suspicion to the proof which already exists (line 10), yet pleads that all his neglect was really a test of the value of the young man's own love (lines 13–14).

The sonnet is full of self-critical words and phrases: 'scanted', 'Forgot', 'frequent been with unknown minds', 'given to time', 'hoisted sail to all the winds' (gone around with everyone and anyone). They are particular examples of the 'wilfulness and errors' which Shakespeare has shown towards his friend.

Sonnet 117 is linked to Sonnet 116 by theme (enduring love, proving a case, measuring the value of love, errors in love), and by the imagery of shipping and law. Try reading them together to see how far you think one echoes and extends the other.

scanted all neglected
deserts favours
bonds duties
unknown minds strangers, nobodies
given to time wasted
dear-purchased lovingly bought

Book write
wilfulness selfishness, lust
on just proof surmise accumulate
  to true evidence add suspicion
level field of fire
prove test

Like as to make our appetites more keen
With eager compounds we our palate urge,
As to prevent our maladies unseen
We sicken to shun sickness when we purge: 4
Even so, being full of your ne'er-cloying sweetness,
To bitter sauces did I frame my feeding,
And, sick of welfare, found a kind of meetness
To be diseased ere that there was true needing.   8
Thus policy in love, t'anticipate
The ills that were not, grew to faults assured,
And brought to medicine a healthful state
Which, rank of goodness, would by ill be cured.   12
     But thence I learn, and find the lesson true,
     Drugs poison him that so fell sick of you.

Shakespeare uses dietary and medical similes to explain why he has been keeping bad company, the 'unknown minds' of Sonnet 117. Just as we sharpen our appetites with spicy sauces, or take unpleasant medicines ('purge') to prevent illness, so Shakespeare has mixed with inferior people ('bitter sauces'). This cunning 'policy' has, however, only made things worse, because he acquired a real sickness ('faults assured'). His previous healthy state was made sick ('brought to medicine').

Shakespeare implies he has learned that letting his affections stray to others is a poison. The couplet makes an ironic joke: love for the young man may be a disease, but it is only a benign illness.

As you read the sonnet, keep in mind the modern medical practice of inoculation, or injecting a mild form of a disease to ensure immunity from the disease. What is your response to the sonnet's argument that love is a sickness?

eager compounds spicy sauces	**ne'er-cloying** never disgusting
our palate urge stimulate our taste	**welfare** health, happiness
maladies unseen potential illnesses	**meetness** appropriateness
shun avoid	**ere that** before
Even so in the same way	**t'anticipate** to prevent

What potions have I drunk of Siren tears
Distilled from limbecks foul as hell within,
Applying fears to hopes, and hopes to fears,
Still losing when I saw myself to win! 4
What wretched errors hath my heart committed,
Whilst it hath thought itself so blessèd never!
How have mine eyes out of their spheres been fitted
In the distraction of this madding fever! 8
O benefit of ill! now I find true
That better is by evil still made better,
And ruined love when it is built anew
Grows fairer than at first, more strong, far greater. 12
    So I return rebuked to my content,
    And gain by ills thrice more than I have spent.

This sonnet continues the theme of Sonnet 118 that improved health can result from sickness, or love can be made stronger by harsh testing. It hints that Shakespeare has been unfaithful: a 'Siren' was a mythical creature, half-woman, half-bird, whose sweet singing lured sailors to their death. A dominant image is that of alchemy, the false science which sought to turn base metal into gold, just as medicine seeks to turn diseased bodies into healthy ones.

After speaking of the 'wretched errors' experienced in the fever of madness, the sonnet finds that there is comfort in such ordeals: 'O benefit of ill!'. Good comes of evil, love is made stronger being broken, and content comes from undergoing the trials of evil or unfaithfulness.

How far do you agree with the sonnet's claims that harsh testing or infidelities strengthen love?

potions drugs
Siren falsely alluring
limbecks containers used by
  alchemists
so blessèd never! never so fortunate

out of ... fitted driven out of their
  sockets by fits
distraction delirium
rebuked chastened

That you were once unkind befriends me now,
And for that sorrow which I then did feel
Needs must I under my transgression bow,
Unless my nerves were brass or hammerèd steel.   4
For if you were by my unkindness shaken
As I by yours, y'have passed a hell of time,
And I, a tyrant, have no leisure taken
To weigh how once I suffered in your crime.   8
O that our night of woe might have rememb'red
My deepest sense, how hard true sorrow hits,
And soon to you, as you to me then, tend'red
The humble salve, which wounded bosoms fits!   12
    But that your trespass now becomes a fee;
    Mine ransoms yours, and yours must ransom me.

Sonnet 120 echoes the earlier sonnets of emotional betrayal, Sonnets 35–6, 40–42 and 92–6. It balances the painful feelings of unfaithfulness on both sides. Match the summary below to the appropriate lines:

Remembering that you were once unkind comforts me. Recalling the pain I felt then saves me from feeling weighed down with guilt for my infidelity, which I would surely feel unless my senses were as hard as steel. You'd feel dreadful if your feelings of betrayal were as painful as mine. Like a tyrant, I failed to recall how I felt when you betrayed me. If only the recollection of that awful time of sorrow had touched my deepest feelings, I would have offered you the healing balm of a soothing apology, as you once apologised to soothe my heart-break. But now your infidelity has become a payment: my wrongdoing pays for yours, and your wrongdoing pays for mine.

Write a sonnet giving the young man's response to this argument.

transgression wrongdoing	**tend'red** willingly gave
hammerèd steel the toughest steel	**humble salve** soothing apologies
shaken emotionally distressed	**trespass** offence
leisure thought, time	**fee** payment
night of woe time of misery	

121

'Tis better to be vile than vile esteemed,
When not to be receives reproach of being,
And the just pleasure lost, which is so deemed
Not by our feeling but by others' seeing. 4
For why should others' false adulterate eyes
Give salutation to my sportive blood?
Or on my frailties why are frailer spies,
Which in their wills count bad what I think good? 8
No, I am that I am, and they that level
At my abuses reckon up their own;
I may be straight though they themselves be bevel;
By their rank thoughts my deeds must not be shown, 12
    Unless this general evil they maintain:
    All men are bad and in their badness reign.

Sonnet 121 argues that it is better to be wicked than to be thought wicked, since rumour-mongers always condemn rightful enjoyment ('just pleasure') as sexual misbehaviour anyway. Those who spread such malicious rumours ('salutation', 'rank thoughts') only reveal their own corruption ('reckon up their own').

Almost every line in the sonnet contains a word or phrase which implies 'rumours' or 'wrongful accusations', for example, 'vile esteemed', 'reproach of being', and so on. Shakespeare defends his integrity against such slanders: 'I am that I am'. He stands up for his own judgement against the judgements of 'frailer spies', those who are more corrupt than he is. What they see as bad, he thinks of as good.

How far do you agree with the following: 'Sonnet 121 presents great difficulties in its details, but its general sense is clear: people who spread rumours reveal their own corruption and cynicism. What they condemn as bad, I know to be good.'

reproach of being the reputation of
 being vile
so deemed thought vile
adulterate corrupt
sportive blood sensuality
Which who

wills desires
level aim, guess
bevel crooked
rank corrupt
maintain propose

Thy gift, thy tables, are within my brain
Full charactered with lasting memory,
Which shall above that idle rank remain
Beyond all date, even to eternity;   4
Or, at the least, so long as brain and heart
Have faculty by nature to subsist,
Till each to razed oblivion yield his part
Of thee, thy record never can be missed.   8
That poor retention could not so much hold,
Nor need I tallies thy dear love to score;
Therefore to give them from me was I bold,
To trust those tables that receive thee more: 12
     To keep an adjunct to remember thee
     Were to import forgetfulness in me.

Shakespeare excuses himself for having given away a notebook ('tables') which was a gift from the young man. He describes the notebook scornfully as of 'idle rank' (lower status, mere jottings).

The notebook is an 'adjunct' or aide-memoire. It is far inferior in value to what is in Shakespeare's brain, that is, thoughts which will last for eternity, or at least as long as brain and heart live. Shakespeare's excuse for giving away the notebook is that keeping it would imply that he would forget the young man without it as a reminder of him.

Sonnet 122 seems to contradict what Shakespeare argues in many other sonnets, the idea that written verses will ensure that the young man's beauty will last for ever. Now he claims that writing is inferior to human memory, and that memory will last only as long as human life, not eternally. To help you with this paradox, turn back to Sonnet 77 and think about whose writing is in the notebook, Shakespeare's or his friend's.

---

charactered inscribed
faculty power, capacity
subsist survive
razed oblivion destructive
 forgetfulness
record memory

That poor retention your notebook
tallies notched sticks used for
 calculations
those tables my memory
import imply, signify

123

No! Time, thou shalt not boast that I do change:
Thy pyramids built up with newer might
To me are nothing novel, nothing strange;
They are but dressings of a former sight. 4
Our dates are brief, and therefore we admire
What thou dost foist upon us that is old,
And rather make them born to our desire
Than think that we before have heard them told. 8
Thy registers and thee I both defy,
Not wond'ring at the present, nor the past,
For thy recòrds, and what we see, doth lie,
Made more or less by thy continual haste. 12
   This I do vow and this shall ever be:
   I will be true despite thy scythe and thee.

Shakespeare again expresses his defiance of Time. He declares that his love will not change, just as nothing in the world really changes. Even the oldest things are 'but dressings of a former sight', merely misleading reappearances of what has been seen before.

Many attempts have been made to set a date when Sonnet 123 was written. For instance, the 'pyramids' in line 2 could be the Egyptian obelisks set up in Rome in the 1580s; the triumphal monuments erected for the coronation of James I in 1603; or the pyramidal columns around the tomb of the Southampton family.

It may be that Shakespeare simply had in mind a general impression of the many newly-erected spires, steeples and conical roofs which he would have seen on buildings in London and around the country.

How far do you agree with the student who said: 'It's about the proverb "there's nothing new under the sun", but it reads unconvincingly, like someone trying to cheer himself up.'?

---

dates lifespans
foist thrust, palm off
born to our desire created by our own ambitions
told spoken about

registers historical records, chronicles
more or less of changing appearance and importance

'Thy pyramids built up with newer might.' Was Shakespeare thinking of the London skyline with which he was so familiar? Or did he visualise the four pyramidal columns around the Southampton family tomb in Titchfield Church, Hampshire? It was erected in 1593 by the third earl, Henry Wriothesley, who may have been the young man of *The Sonnets*. (He is the kneeling figure on the right.) Perhaps Shakespeare had an image in mind of the Egyptian pyramids. They were the most ancient structures then known, and for many Elizabethans they represented the very beginning of time.

124

If my dear love were but the child of state,
It might for Fortune's bastard be unfathered,
As subject to Time's love, or to Time's hate,
Weeds among weeds, or flowers with flowers gathered.   4
No, it was builded far from accident;
It suffers not in smiling pomp, nor falls
Under the blow of thrallèd discontent,
Whereto th'inviting time our fashion calls;   8
It fears not Policy, that heretic,
Which works on leases of short-numb'red hours,
But all alone stands hugely politic,
That it nor grows with heat, nor drowns with show'rs.   12
    To this I witness call the fools of Time,
    Which die for goodness, who have lived for crime.

Shakespeare rejects any idea that his love is influenced by circumstances. It does not fluctuate with chance ('Fortune', 'accident') or with Time. Neither is it affected by the flattery of the great ('smiling pomp'), by melancholy or by resentment ('thrallèd discontent').

Love is not subject to self-interest or 'Policy', which satisfies the needs of the moment and works only for 'leases of short-numb'red hours' (short-term gain). If it were such a 'child of state' (self-seeking product of circumstance), it would deserve to be disowned or 'unfathered'. In lines 11–12, Shakespeare declares his love to be 'hugely politic', supremely wise and never changing, whatever the circumstances.

Sonnet 124 has been described as having 'beautiful complexity', and as 'so much greater than the sum of its parts'. The interpretations given above and opposite explore only a tiny fraction of the sonnet's possibilities. Use them as starting points for your own responses.

---

dear love sincere devotion
builded ... accident not the
  outcome of chance
thrallèd discontent melancholy,
  bottled-up discontent

Whereto th'inviting time ... calls
  to which today's temptations lure
  people like us
heretic unfaithful disbeliever, deviant
witness call call as witnesses

a Sonnet 124 echoes Sonnet 116 both in its imagery and in its attempt to define the nature of 'dear love'. Read the two sonnets in succession to discover how they both assert the unchanging nature of love.

b Line 4 has been described as Shakespeare's mature style at its best. One interpretation is that Time is so capricious (changeable) that it produces useless weeds (from 'Time's hate'), as well as cherished flowers (from 'Time's love'). A more searching interpretation is that Shakespeare claims his love to be unique; it is distinctive and special. If it were just the product of circumstance, a 'child of state', it would be like every other love, as indistinguishable as 'weeds among weeds', or 'flowers with flowers'. All are cut down indiscriminately in bundles ('gathered'), just as Time's scythe reaps and destroys all ordinary loves.

c Many attempts have been made to identify the 'fools of Time' in lines 13–14. They are witnesses on whom Shakespeare wished to call to illustrate his theme that love is not 'Policy' (expediency or self-interest). Their example would show that only such time-servers or dupes of time change sides or beliefs to achieve short-term gain or to fit in with current circumstances.

They could be those who, having lived a life of crime, repent on their deathbeds, in the hope of entering heaven. Or they could be those who, about to be executed for terrorism, denounce their crimes. They may be those who die as martyrs for a cause of which the ruling class disapproves. But the line could also mean those who, having lived a life of crime, are justly executed.

Did Shakespeare have actual people in mind as 'the fools of Time'? Some critics argue that he did not, and that to try to identify an actual group diminishes the sonnet's celebration of a love which defies historical change. Others argue that identification of a particular group can increase understanding and enjoyment of the sonnet. All of the following suggestions have been made:

- The Protestant martyrs who were burnt at the stake in the reign of Queen Mary (Foxe's Martyrs).
- The Catholics (Jesuits) who were executed in the reign of Queen Elizabeth, particularly in the years 1594–5.
- The Earl of Essex and his followers, whose rebellion failed in 1601.
- Guy Fawkes and his comrades who tried to blow up the Houses of Parliament in 1605.

You may want to research some of the above to discover if such knowledge deepens your appreciation of Sonnet 124.

Were't aught to me I bore the canopy,
With my extern the outward honouring,
Or laid great bases for eternity,
Which proves more short than waste or ruining?   4
Have I not seen dwellers on form and favour
Lose all, and more, by paying too much rent,
For compound sweet forgoing simple savour,
Pitiful thrivers, in their gazing spent?   8
No, let me be obsequious in thy heart,
And take thou my oblation, poor but free,
Which is not mixed with seconds, knows no art
But mutual render, only me for thee.   12
    Hence, thou suborned informer! A true soul
    When most impeached stands least in thy control.

Shakespeare rejects the public displays of honour and status, such as carrying the canopy under which a monarch walks, or building great houses to last for eternity. These external shows of love prove short-lived. They ruin the flattering courtiers ('dwellers on form and favour', 'Pitiful thrivers') who seek social advancement by such methods. All he values in their place is a heartfelt and sincere exchange of love ('mutual render').

The couplet banishes the 'suborned informer' (bribed witness), who has made the accusation that Shakespeare's love is merely the pursuit of social status or wealth.

An emphatic 'no' rings through Sonnets 123, 124 and 125, rejecting the thought that love will change, that it is only self-seeking flattery, or the product of circumstance. Re-read all three sonnets to remind yourself of all the accusations rejected by Shakespeare in each.

Were't aught to me was it anything to me that
great bases gigantic foundations
compound sweet artificial sweetness, false compliments
simple savour natural flavours, plain truth

gazing false adoring looks
obsequious dutiful, devoted
oblation offering, praise
seconds flattery, inferior material
impeached accused, maligned

126

O thou my lovely boy, who in thy power
Dost hold Time's fickle glass, his sickle, hour;
Who hast by waning grown, and therein show'st
Thy lovers withering, as thy sweet self grow'st;   4
If Nature (sovereign mistress over wrack),
As thou goest onwards still will pluck thee back,
She keeps thee to this purpose, that her skill
May Time disgrace, and wretched minutes kill.   8
Yet fear her, O thou minion of her pleasure,
She may detain, but not still keep, her treasure!
    Her audit (though delayed) answered must be,
    And her quietus is to render thee.   12

Sonnet 126 begins by claiming that the young man has power over Time, and is able to prevent or delay ('hold') its destructive nature. He has 'by waning grown', become more beautiful as he grew older, in striking contrast to the marks of age ('withering') on his friends. Nature keeps him in order to defy and disgrace Time, but can only delay death, not defeat it. Inevitably, like the payment of a bill, Nature must finally surrender the young man to death.

Sonnet 126 has only twelve lines. It rhymes in couplets: AA, BB, CC, and so on. Shakespeare may have intended this deliberate departure from the sonnet form as an *envoi* or 'farewell' poem to mark the end of the sequence of sonnets to the young man.

a Suggest how this sonnet makes a suitable conclusion to the sequence of Sonnets 1–126. Consider form, content, themes, imagery, tone and diction.

b Do you think that the sonnet could be read as the fading of Shakespeare's love for the young man?

---

fickle glass ever-changing hour-glass
sickle, hour death (the time when Death's sickle strikes) ,
waning decreasing
wrack decay, destruction

pluck pull, seize
minion favourite, slave
audit final account
quietus quittance, final payment
render surrender

Sonnets 1–126

Henry Wriothesley, Earl of Southampton (1573–1624), was well known for his interest in theatre and the arts. Shakespeare dedicated two poems to him, 'Venus and Adonis', and 'The Rape of Lucrece'. His initials, reversed, are W.H. (see page 6). Other poets competed for the Earl's patronage (see 'rival poet' on pages 93 and 101).

William Herbert, Earl of Pembroke (1580–1630). His initials fit the dedication in *The Sonnets*. As a young man, he was unwilling to marry (see Sonnets 1–17), but had a much-publicised affair with Mary Fitton (see pages 147–8). Pembroke was a patron of Shakespeare, and was acknowledged in the introduction to the First Folio edition of Shakespeare's plays.

Sonnets 1–126 portray the young man as beautiful, but also as unfaithful, neglectful, selfish and cold-hearted. He may have been the 'Mr W.H.' referred to in the dedication (see page 6). Many other identifications have been suggested, but no one really knows who he was.

Sonnets 127–54

Sonnets 1–126 are addressed to a young man, Shakespeare's friend. From Sonnet 127 onwards, a fresh sequence begins, containing sonnets mainly about a woman who has come to be known as 'the dark lady'. Shakespeare reveals his very mixed feelings for this woman, who does not match the conventional image of the blonde-haired, blue-eyed, pale-skinned beauty celebrated in sonnets by earlier poets.

The dark lady is portrayed as being younger than Shakespeare, and not beautiful by the standards of the time. She is promiscuous, a lover of Shakespeare, the young man, and other men. Various suggestions have been made as to her identity, including:

Mary Fitton Mary had a son by William Herbert (see opposite), and was a maid of honour to Queen Elizabeth I. There is a contemporary portrait of her on page 148.

Luce Morgan Also known as Lucy Negro, who was fined and imprisoned for owning a brothel in Clerkenwell.

Emilia Lanier Daughter of a musician at Queen Elizabeth's court, Emilia was the mistress of Lord Hunsdon who, for a time, was the patron of Shakespeare's acting company, the Lord Chamberlain's Men. She wrote and published religious poetry in which she defended the equality of women.

Other strongly argued suggestions for the dark lady include: Queen Elizabeth I; Jacqueline Field, the wife of a friend of Shakespeare; Penelope Devereux, the 'Stella' of Sidney's *Astrophil and Stella*; and even Anne Hathaway, Shakespeare's wife (Sonnet 145 is thought to be about her).

Whoever she was, real or imagined, the dark lady prompted some of Shakespeare's most anguished poetry. Yet his sonnets to her are far from complimentary; Shakespeare criticises her morality, her looks, and even her bad breath! As you read the sonnets about the dark lady, consider some or all of the following:

a Do you think that Shakespeare was genuinely in love with the dark lady, or was the relationship only sexual?

b Did Shakespeare intend her to read Sonnets 127–54?

c How have attitudes to beauty changed since *The Sonnets* were written?

d Do you think that the dark lady really existed, or are the sonnets to her simply literary exercises?

The dark lady of *The Sonnets*? Mary Fitton, a maid of honour to Queen Elizabeth I, has been suggested as the dark-complexioned woman who caused Shakespeare so much emotional agony.

In the old age black was not counted fair,
Or if it were it bore not beauty's name;
But now is black beauty's successive heir,
And beauty slandered with a bastard shame: 4
For since each hand hath put on Nature's power,
Fairing the foul with art's false borrowed face,
Sweet beauty hath no name, no holy bower,
But is profaned, if not lives in disgrace.   8
Therefore my mistress' eyes are raven black,
Her eyes so suited, and they mourners seem
At such who not born fair no beauty lack,
Sland'ring creation with a false esteem: 12
   Yet so they mourn, becoming of their woe,
   That every tongue says beauty should look so.

Sonnet 127 contrasts an earlier time, 'the old age' when black was thought to be incompatible with beauty, with a change in fashion. Now black *is* beautiful. Such a change did in fact take place in the 1590s.

Lines 4–8 roundly condemn cosmetics; painting one's face is seen as 'beauty slandered', 'bastard shame', 'art's false borrowed face'. It debases the 'name' (reputation) and 'holy bower' (sacred dwelling-place) of beauty. In lines 9–12, Shakespeare draws his conclusion that the beauty of his dark-featured mistress is a criticism of those who use cosmetics, thus slandering what 'creation' (nature) intends. Her dark beauty is so 'becoming' or attractive, that everyone now sees it as the model of what beauty should be.

Some critics claim that the alliteration and assonance in line 6 echo the very artificiality of cosmetics which the sonnet is condemning. Do you find their claim convincing?

bore … name was not called beautiful
successive legitimate
each hand … power everybody changes their appearance
Fairing making beautiful

bower sanctuary, dwelling place
profaned desecrated, violated
suited matching
becoming of their woe looking so graceful in grief

128

How oft, when thou, my music, music play'st
Upon that blessèd wood whose motion sounds
With thy sweet fingers when thou gently sway'st
The wiry concord that mine ear confounds,　　　　4
Do I envỳ those jacks that nimble leap
To kiss the tender inward of thy hand,
Whilst my poor lips, which should that harvest reap,
At the wood's boldness by thee blushing stand!　　　8
To be so tickled they would change their state
And situation with those dancing chips
O'er whom thy fingers walk with gentle gait,
Making dead wood more blest than living lips.　　　12
　　Since saucy jacks so happy are in this,
　　Give them thy fingers, me thy lips to kiss.

Sonnet 128 conjures up a picture of the dark lady playing on the virginals with Shakespeare standing beside her, envying the familiar contact the instrument's keys make with her hands. Virginals are a keyboard instrument like a small harpsichord. The keys are described in the sonnet as 'blessèd wood', 'jacks', 'dancing chips', 'dead wood' and 'saucy jacks'.

Some critics think that the sonnet is artificial. They argue that a keyboard instrument is inappropriate to the kissing metaphor; the image of 'harvest' (line 7) is unsupported; keys do not kiss the 'inward' (palm) of the hand; lips do not blush. Those who defend the sonnet's quality claim that the sincerity and genuineness of a real experience come through. They argue that such criticisms are mistaken because they are too literal.

Imagine that you have been invited to comment on these two opposed viewpoints of the sonnet's worth. What will you say?

my music the dark lady (see also Sonnet 8)
blessèd wood fortunate keys (of the virginals)
motion movement
sway'st control

wiry concord harmony (from plucked wire strings)
confounds delights, amazes
state And situation nature and place

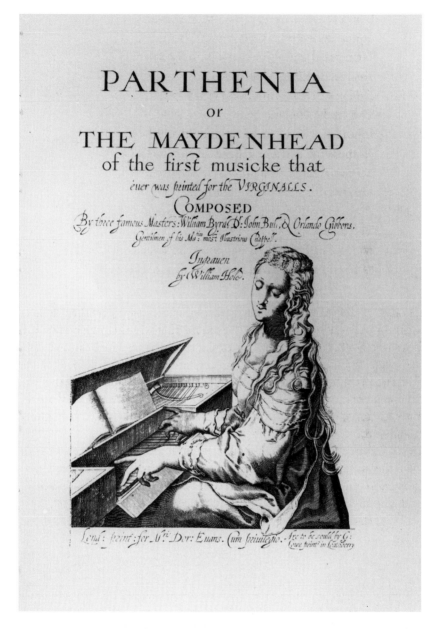

PARTHENIA
or
THE MAYDENHEAD
of the first musicke that
euer was printed for the VIRGINALLS.
COMPOSED
By three famous Masters: William Byrd Dr: John Bull, & Orlando Gibbons.
Gentilmen of his Ma:ties most Illustrious Chappell.

Ingrauen
by William Hole.

Lend: print: for Mrs: Dor: Euans. (um priuilegio. Are to be sould by G:
Loue print in Cradberry

The Sonnets were published in 1609. Only two years later, this book of music for the virginals appeared. The music was composed by three famous royal chapel masters: William Byrd, Dr John Bull and Orlando Gibbons.

Th'expense of spirit in a waste of shame
Is lust in action, and till action, lust
Is perjured, murd'rous, bloody, full of blame,
Savage, extreme, rude, cruel, not to trust,   4
Enjoyed no sooner but despisèd straight,
Past reason hunted, and no sooner had,
Past reason hated as a swallowed bait
On purpose laid to make the taker mad: 8
Mad in pursuit, and in possession so,
Had, having, and in quest to have, extreme,
A bliss in proof, and proved, a very woe,
Before, a joy proposed, behind, a dream.   12
　All this the world well knows, yet none knows well
　To shun the heaven that leads men to this hell.

Sonnet 129 expresses extreme revulsion at the experience and consequences of lust. It charts the frantic and maddened anticipation of lustful sex (lines 3–4), and the desolation of guilt and shame which immediately follows ('despisèd straight', 'Past reason hated', 'a very woe', 'hell'). Like poisoned bait, lust drives people to insanity. Every aspect of lust is extreme: before, during and afterwards. What seems to promise joy proves only an illusion, a dream which is a nightmare of sorrow, self-loathing and despair.

Experiment with ways of reading the sonnet to bring out the sense of loathing and revulsion, the swings of feeling in the anticipation and consequence of 'lust in action', and the frenetic, tumbling, rapid pace of thoughts.

Does the sonnet sound convincing if you read it aloud slowly, as if you were coolly working through a logical argument?

expense squandering
spirit vitality, spirituality, semen
waste of shame shameful orgy
perjured lying
blame guilt, harm
Past reason irrationally

bait trap
quest seeking
proof test, experience
a very woe a real cause of revulsion
dream nightmare

My mistress' eyes are nothing like the sun;
Coral is far more red than her lips' red;
If snow be white, why then her breasts are dun;
If hairs be wires, black wires grow on her head.   4
I have seen roses damasked, red and white,
But no such roses see I in her cheeks,
And in some perfumes is there more delight
Than in the breath that from my mistress reeks.   8
I love to hear her speak, yet well I know
That music hath a far more pleasing sound;
I grant I never saw a goddess go –
My mistress when she walks treads on the ground.   12
    And yet, by heaven, I think my love as rare
    As any she belied with false compare.

Sonnet 130 mocks the Elizabethan sonnet tradition, in which poets extravagantly praised their mistresses, comparing their beauty to the sun, to roses, or to harmonious music. Shakespeare rejects such exaggerated comparisons (hyperbole), just as he had rejected them in Sonnet 21. He deliberately uses an 'unpoetic' word, 'reeks', and emphasises that his mistress 'treads on the ground' like any other human being.

Shakespeare refuses to compare his mistress to the sun, to coral, to white snow, or to the fine gold thread ('wires') used in Elizabethan jewellery. In doing so, he questions the use of metaphor and simile in poetry, because they untruthfully and dishonestly glorify other women, 'As any she belied with false compare'. The dark lady is beautiful ('as rare') without these hollow and spurious comparisons.

Decide whether or not you think that Shakespeare intended his mistress to see Sonnet 130. What might she have thought if she had read it?

---

dun grey
damasked dappled (mingled
  colours)
go walk

rare extraordinary, valuable,
  incomparable
belied wrongly praised, lied about
  (see also Sonnet 21)

131

Thou art as tyrannous, so as thou art,
As those whose beauties proudly make them cruel;
For well thou know'st to my dear doting heart
Thou art the fairest and most precious jewel.   4
Yet in good faith some say that thee behold,
Thy face hath not the power to make love groan;
To say they err, I dare not be so bold,
Although I swear it to myself alone.   8
And to be sure that is not false I swear,
A thousand groans but thinking on thy face
One on another's neck do witness bear
Thy black is fairest in my judgement's place.   12
   In nothing art thou black save in thy deeds,
   And thence this slander as I think proceeds.

Shakespeare admits to being besotted by his dark-featured mistress. Although others do not find her conventionally beautiful, to him she is 'the fairest and most precious jewel'. Merely thinking of her face makes him sigh continually. In Shakespeare's mind, her dark beauty is the best, 'fairest in my judgement's place'.

However, the sonnet ends with the recognition that the dark lady is far from perfect in her morality and behaviour. She is as tyrannous as the cruel, beautiful women of conventional sonnets (lines 1–2), and her deeds are 'black' (line 13). In Elizabethan times, the word 'black' was very negative, signifying both ugliness and immoral behaviour.

One critic described the phrase 'as I think' (line 14) as 'transforming the whole couplet into a single graceful razor stroke'. To what extent do you agree with his judgement that Shakespeare is savagely, if elegantly, critical of his mistress?

tyrannous cruel and pitiless
so as thou art just as you are (not beautiful)
dear doting tender and madly devoted
to make love groan to make a lover sigh

err are mistaken
but thinking when I only think
One on another's neck one sigh quickly following another
judgement's place mind, feeling

Thine eyes I love, and they, as pitying me,
Knowing thy heart torment me with disdain,
Have put on black, and loving mourners be,
Looking with pretty ruth upon my pain.   4
And truly not the morning sun of heaven
Better becomes the grey cheeks of the east,
Nor that full star that ushers in the even
Doth half that glory to the sober west   8
As those two mourning eyes become thy face.
O let it then as well beseem thy heart
To mourn for me, since mourning doth thee grace,
And suit thy pity like in every part.   12
    Then will I swear beauty herself is black,
    And all they foul that thy complexion lack.

Sonnet 132 shows that the dark lady is giving Shakespeare a hard time, treating him with disdain. He pleads with her to match the pity shown in her eyes with similar compassion in her heart. In the closing couplet, he claims that, if she does so, he will swear that perfect beauty is black, and all other complexions are ugly or 'foul'.

a The sonnet does not conform to the usual structure of lines (4 + 4 + 4 + 2). Work out the form of its four sections.

b The theme of eyes and hearts and a pun on 'morning'/'mourning' runs through the sonnet. Lines 5–9 compare the dark lady's face to 'the morning sun of heaven' and to 'that full star' (Venus, the evening star). Imagine that you asked Shakespeare to consider those comparisons in the light of Sonnet 130, in which he condemned such poetic hyperbole (exaggerated praise). What would he say in reply?

Have put on have dressed in
ruth pity, compassion
becomes befits, is suited to
ushers in the even announces evening
Doth does, gives

beseem become, match, grace
suit dress
like in every part alike throughout your being
complexion features, nature

Beshrew that heart that makes my heart to groan
For that deep wound it gives my friend and me!
Is't not enough to torture me alone,
But slave to slavery my sweet'st friend must be? 4
Me from myself thy cruel eye hath taken,
And my next self thou harder hast engrossed:
Of him, myself, and thee I am forsaken,
A torment thrice threefold thus to be crossed. 8
Prison my heart in thy steel bosom's ward,
But then my friend's heart let my poor heart bail;
Whoe'er keeps me, let my heart be his guard,
Thou canst not then use rigour in my jail. 12
    And yet thou wilt, for I, being pent in thee,
    Perforce am thine, and all that is in me.

Sonnet 133 reveals that the dark lady has stolen the love of Shakespeare's friend, the young man of Sonnets 1–126. Just as she tortured Shakespeare, she now enslaves the young man's affections. Shakespeare feels a three-fold loss: his own being, his friend ('my next self'), and the dark lady herself. He knows that his plea to guard his friend's heart from her cruelty is of no avail. She imprisons him, so that everything within him (his love for the young man) becomes hers.

The image of slavery was conventional in the stories and poems of the Romance Tradition on which Shakespeare drew. In that tradition, a beautiful lady was cruel to her lovers, who were often close friends. They regarded themselves as her devoted servants.

The relationship described in the sonnet is a variation of the 'eternal triangle'. There are over thirty mentions of the three people involved. As you read the sonnet, quietly emphasise each (for example, 'that heart' and 'my heart' in line 1).

Beshrew curse
taken captured, stolen
harder more cruelly
engrossed trapped, debased
forsaken deprived
crossed thwarted

steel bosom's ward hard heart's prison cell
bail release, confine
rigour harshness, cruelty
pent imprisoned
Perforce necessarily

134

So now I have confessed that he is thine,
And I myself am mortgaged to thy will,
Myself I'll forfeit, so that other mine
Thou wilt restore to be my comfort still: 4
But thou wilt not, nor he will not be free,
For thou art covetous, and he is kind;
He learned but surety-like to write for me
Under that bond that him as fast doth bind.   8
The statute of thy beauty thou wilt take,
Thou usurer, that put'st forth all to use,
And sue a friend came debtor for my sake,
So him I lose through my unkind abuse.   12
    Him have I lost, thou hast both him and me;
    He pays the whole, and yet am I not free.

This sonnet follows on from Sonnet 133, acknowledging that the dark lady has enslaved both men. Shakespeare offers to exchange ('forfeit') himself in return for the young man ('that other mine'), although he knows that neither the dark lady nor the young man will agree.

It seems that the love-triangle developed when the young man acted as a go-between ('surety-like'), wooing the dark lady on Shakespeare's behalf. But the young man fell in love with her and now is held 'fast' by the bonds of love. She, like a harsh money-lender ('usurer'), uses everything for her own interest ('use'). In lines 13–14, Shakespeare admits that he has lost the young man, and that he, too, is in love with the dark lady.

a Financial and legal metaphors pervade the sonnet. Pick out all such words or phrases, for example, 'mortgaged', 'forfeit' and 'restore'.

b The sonnet contains sexual implications which become explicit in Sonnets 135 and 136. Re-read this sonnet after the next two sonnets.

So Well, following my conclusion in Sonnet 133
mortgaged pledged (as a security liable to forfeit)
will desire
restore give back

still always
covetous selfish, greedy
kind benevolent, considerate
bond contract
statute mortgage deed, legal rights
came debtor who became a debtor

Whoever hath her wish, thou hast thy Will,
And Will to boot, and Will in overplus;
More than enough am I that vex thee still,
To thy sweet will making addition thus.   4
Wilt thou, whose will is large and spacious,
Not once vouchsafe to hide my will in thine?
Shall will in others seem right gracious,
And in my will no fair acceptance shine?   8
The sea, all water, yet receives rain still,
And in abundance addeth to his store;
So thou being rich in Will add to thy Will
One will of mine to make thy large Will more.   12
    Let no unkind, no fair beseechers kill;
    Think all but one, and me in that one Will.

Sonnet 135 seems to be a plea to the dark lady to include Shakespeare among her many lovers. It should be read together with Sonnet 136. They are full of puns on the word 'will', which is used twenty times in the two sonnets.

Some editors and readers have ignored the sexual implications of Sonnets 135 and 136, thinking them obscene. However, it is very likely that Shakespeare and his male friends enjoyed such sexual joking. Many modern comedians use similar punning techniques to get laughs. As you read the two sonnets, keep in mind the following possible meanings of 'will':

William Shakespeare	sexual desire, lust
the name of the young man	the male sexual organ
the dark lady's husband	the female sexual organ
wish: the desire to do or have something	what will happen in the future
wilfulness: the desire to have one's own way	

---

to boot in addition
overplus excess
vex trouble, irritate
vouchsafe grant, agree

store abundant stock
no unkind, no fair beseechers neither cruel and ungenerous lovers, nor honourable lovers (or flatterers)

If thy soul check thee that I come so near,
Swear to thy blind soul that I was thy Will,
And will thy soul knows is admitted there;
Thus far for love, my love-suit, sweet, fulfil.   4
Will will fulfil the treasure of thy love,
Ay, fill it full with wills, and my will one.
In things of great receipt with ease we prove
Among a number one is reckoned none: 8
Then in the number let me pass untold,
Though in thy store's account I one must be;
For nothing hold me, so it please thee hold
That nothing me, a something sweet to thee.   12
    Make but my name thy love, and love that still,
    And then thou lovest me for my name is Will.

The sexual innuendoes (double-meanings) of Sonnet 135 continue, and this sonnet adds another, as 'nothing' was the Elizabethan slang for the female sexual organ. Shakespeare again pleads to become one of the dark lady's many lovers. In line 8, he echoes a common proverb of the time ('one is no number'), saying that one more lover will make no difference to her list of lovers ('store's account'). Line 14 is often taken as evidence that Shakespeare is revealing his identity ('my name is Will'), but not everyone believes that!

a Imagine that you have been invited to discuss Sonnets 135 and 136 with either a group of fellow students, or university professors, or a church group, or on a televised discussion programme. Choose your audience and prepare a list of the points you intend to make.

b If you had to give a public reading of Sonnets 135 and 136, how would you speak them?

---

soul conscience
check rebuke, punish
I come so near I tell the truth about
  you, I'm too close
blind unseeing, ignorant

love-suit pleas of love, advances
treasure female sexual organ
great receipt great value, huge
  capacity, great importance
untold uncounted, in secret

Thou blind fool, Love, what dost thou to mine eyes,
That they behold, and see not what they see?
They know what beauty is, see where it lies,
Yet what the best is take the worst to be.   4
If eyes, corrupt by over-partial looks,
Be anchored in the bay where all men ride,
Why of eyes' falsehood hast thou forgèd hooks,
Whereto the judgement of my heart is tied?   8
Why should my heart think that a several plot,
Which my heart knows the wide world's common place?
Or mine eyes seeing this, say this is not,
To put fair truth upon so foul a face?   12
  In things right true my heart and eyes have erred,
  And to this false plague are they now transferred.

Shakespeare questions what infatuation has done to his eyes, making him see beauty in a woman whose appearance and deeds are far from beautiful or moral. His lying eyes corrupt his judgement; he sees 'fair truth' in 'so foul a face', and denies the reality which confronts him. Why? Because his heart and his eyes have caught a 'false plague', mistaking what is 'right true'.

The sonnet contains savage condemnation of the sexual promiscuity of the dark lady. She is everybody's and anybody's, 'the bay where all men ride', and 'the wide world's common place'. These two wounding images may tell you more about Shakespeare's feelings than about the dark lady's nature. Do you find them:

- nasty or witty?

- sexist metaphors, typical of what men say about women?

- hypocritical, in that they condemn women for promiscuity, but make no such judgement on men who do the same?

---

blind fool Cupid (the god of love, a blind boy)
lies lives, deceives, rests
over-partial prejudiced, infatuated, biased
forgèd made in steel

several plot private place
common place public grounds (anybody's)
erred been mistaken
transferred changed, removed

When my love swears that she is made of truth,
I do believe her, though I know she lies,
That she might think me some untutored youth,
Unlearnèd in the world's false subtleties.   4
Thus vainly thinking that she thinks me young,
Although she knows my days are past the best,
Simply I credit her false-speaking tongue:
On both sides thus is simple truth suppressed.   8
But wherefore says she not she is unjust?
And wherefore say not I that I am old?
O love's best habit is in seeming trust,
And age in love loves not t'have years told.   12
  Therefore I lie with her, and she with me,
  And in our faults by lies we flattered be.

Sonnet 138 can be read as an answer to the problem posed in lines 9–10 as to why people don't tell each other the truth. It expresses the mutual deception and hypocrisy ('seeming trust') by which lovers can keep their relationship intact. The sonnet puns on the double meaning of 'lie', namely to tell untruths or to sleep with. Lying to, and with, each other may be 'faults', but they give pleasure.

Shakespeare does not believe that the dark lady is honest in language or in love. Nonetheless, he pretends to believe her so that she will think him inexperienced and young, 'some untutored youth'. But he knows that she knows that he is old and doesn't wish to be reminded of his age!

The tone of the sonnet has been described as both 'downright smug' and 'delightfully ironic'. Think about these two judgements, then suggest how you would describe the sonnet's tone.

---

made of truth honest, faithful
subtleties ways of behaving
vainly out of vanity
Simply foolishly, naïvely
credit pretend to believe

suppressed hidden
unjust lying, unfaithful
habit custom
seeming trust pretending to trust
told counted, revealed

139

O call not me to justify the wrong
That thy unkindness lays upon my heart;
Wound me not with thine eye but with thy tongue;
Use power with power, and slay me not by art.   4
Tell me thou lov'st elsewhere; but in my sight,
Dear heart, forbear to glance thine eye aside;
What need'st thou wound with cunning when thy might
Is more than my o'erpressed defence can bide?   8
Let me excuse thee: 'Ah, my love well knows
Her pretty looks have been mine enemies,
And therefore from my face she turns my foes,
That they elsewhere might dart their injuries.'   12
    Yet do not so, but since I am near slain,
    Kill me outright with looks, and rid my pain.

In the sonnet tradition (see page 178), it was customary for a lover to justify and excuse the cruelty he received at the hands of a disdainful woman. In this sonnet, Shakespeare seems to overturn the tradition, rejecting such justification (line 1).

Shakespeare pleads with the dark lady to tell him of her affairs with other men, and not to look at others when he is with her. The wounds she inflicts with her eyes are worse than anything she can say. The 'wounding' image is continued in the couplet, as Shakespeare demands that she end his misery by killing him outright with looks (like the basilisk or mythical dragon-like beast, which killed with its eyes).

Lines 9–12 ('Ah, my love … injuries') are often claimed to be deliberately insincere and contrived, using artificial language to ridicule the language found in conventional sonnets ('pretty looks', 'enemies', and so on). Contrast the lines in tone, vocabulary and meaning with lines 13–14.

Use power with power use direct force, fight fairly
art strategy, cunning
What need'st thou why bother to
might power over me

o'erpressed strongly attacked, too hard pressed
bide endure
my foes (the dark lady's eyes)

Be wise as thou art cruel, do not press
My tongue-tied patience with too much disdain,
Lest sorrow lend me words, and words express
The manner of my pity-wanting pain.   4
If I might teach thee wit, better it were,
Though not to love, yet, love, to tell me so –
As testy sick men, when their deaths be near,
No news but health from their physicians know.   8
For if I should despair, I should grow mad,
And in my madness might speak ill of thee;
Now this ill-wresting world is grown so bad,
Mad slanderers by mad ears believèd be.   12
    That I may not be so, nor thou belied,
    Bear thine eyes straight, though thy proud heart go wide.

Sonnet 140 adds to the pleading of the previous sonnet, echoing its vocabulary and theme. It urges the dark lady to look only on the poet, even if she loves others. Using the image of irritable sick men who are told only good news by their doctors, Shakespeare asks the dark lady to tell him that she loves him, even if she doesn't (lines 5–8).

The sonnet seems to say: if you don't pity me, my sorrow will make me mad and speak ill of you, and those slanders will be believed by others. Is this a warning to the dark lady that Shakespeare is likely to slander her? Is it a direct threat, a piece of genuine advice, a sorrowful plea or a combination of all these?

Experiment with different ways of speaking the sonnet to discover an appropriate tone (or tones).

---

press attack, oppress, injure
pity-wanting unpitied
wit wisdom
testy irritable

ill-wresting lying, truth-twisting,
  slanderous
belied slandered
Bear ... wide look at me, even
  though you love others

141

In faith, I do not love thee with mine eyes,
For they in thee a thousand errors note,
But 'tis my heart that loves what they despise,
Who in despite of view is pleased to dote.   4
Nor are mine ears with thy tongue's tune delighted,
Nor tender feeling to base touches prone,
Nor taste, nor smell, desire to be invited
To any sensual feast with thee alone;   8
But my five wits nor my five senses can
Dissuade one foolish heart from serving thee,
Who leaves unswayed the likeness of a man,
Thy proud heart's slave and vassal wretch to be.   12
    Only my plague thus far I count my gain,
    That she that makes me sin awards me pain.

Sonnet 141 shows how much Shakespeare's body and mind are enslaved by the dark lady. Although his eyes see 'a thousand errors' in her appearance and behaviour, his heart 'is pleased to dote'. He loves her passionately, even though his five senses (sight, sound, touch, taste and smell) find fault with her.

Neither his senses nor his five wits (common sense, imagination, fantasy, evaluation, memory) can inhibit his love. His heart, given to such abject slavery, ceases to govern ('leaves unswayed') his being, leaving him a mere shell ('the likeness of a man'). But the couplet finds some comfort in the 'plague' of love, and there is even some satisfaction in the pain she causes him.

The sonnet gives full expression to the opposition of eye and heart developed in the preceding four sonnets. You can also find sustained explorations of the same theme in Sonnets 24, 46–7, 93 and 132–3.

In faith truly
errors blemishes (physical and moral)
in despite of view in spite of what I see
dote love passionately

thy tongue's tune the sound of your voice
base touches prone responsive to sexual advances
vassal wretch poor servant
sin (see Sonnet 142)

Love is my sin, and thy dear virtue hate,
Hate of my sin, grounded on sinful loving.
O but with mine compare thou thine own state,
And thou shalt find it merits not reproving,   4
Or if it do, not from those lips of thine,
That have profaned their scarlet ornaments,
And sealed false bonds of love as oft as mine,
Robbed others' beds' revènues of their rents.   8
Be it lawful I love thee as thou lov'st those
Whom thine eyes woo as mine impòrtune thee:
Root pity in thy heart, that when it grows
Thy pity may deserve to pitied be.   12
    If thou dost seek to have what thou dost hide,
    By self-example mayst thou be denied.

Sonnet 142 seems to charge the dark lady with hypocrisy. It rebukes her for condemning Shakespeare's love. She is in no position to criticise, because she herself is guilty of sexual infidelity. If Shakespeare is hated for 'sinful loving', her 'state' is the same.

In the second quatrain, the metaphor of a property contract sealed with red wax conveys a direct accusation, that the dark lady has stolen other women's husbands ('Robbed others' beds' revènues of their rents'). Some readers feel that this metaphor so debases the relationship that Shakespeare is undermining his own argument. Do you agree?

Lines 11–14 plead for pity, which, if given, will be extended to her. The couplet could be spoken in very different tones. Try speaking it as a threat, as a friendly warning, and as a matter-of-fact statement.

grounded on based upon
it merits not reproving it doesn't deserve condemnation
profaned defiled, mocked
scarlet ornaments blushes, dignity
bonds promises, contracts

Robbed ... rents committed adultery with other women's husbands
impòrtune plead with
what thou dost hide what you hold back (pity)

Lo, as a careful huswife runs to catch
One of her feathered creatures broke away,
Sets down her babe and makes all swift dispatch
In pùrsuit of the thing she would have stay,   4
Whilst her neglected child holds her in chase,
Cries to catch her whose busy care is bent
To follow that which flies before her face,
Not prizing her poor infant's discontent: 8
So runn'st thou after that which flies from thee,
Whilst I, thy babe, chase thee afar behind;
But if thou catch thy hope, turn back to me,
And play the mother's part, kiss me, be kind.   12
    So will I pray that thou mayst have thy Will,
    If thou turn back and my loud crying still.

Sonnet 143 uses a domestic image to present a view of the love-triangle in which Shakespeare was caught. Just as a housewife pursues an escaped chicken and her neglected child runs crying after her, so the dark lady pursues another man, whilst Shakespeare, neglected, longs for the comfort of her love.

On account of its simplicity and ordinariness, some critics have questioned whether Sonnet 143 was really written by Shakespeare. Others argue that it is genuinely Shakespearean, and find poetic value in its theme, its position in the sonnet sequence 133–44, its language and its imagery. Consider each of these four elements in turn, make your own judgement about the sonnet's quality, and about whether or not you think it was written by Shakespeare.

huswife housewife (pronounced
  'hussif')
all swift dispatch haste
holds her in chase chases her

bent directed
prizing regarding, valuing
still stop, calm

Two loves I have, of comfort and despair,
Which like two spirits do suggest me still:
The better angel is a man right fair;
The worser spirit a woman coloured ill.   4
To win me soon to hell my female evil
Tempteth my better angel from my side,
And would corrupt my saint to be a devil,
Wooing his purity with her foul pride.   8
And whether that my angel be turned fiend
Suspect I may, yet not directly tell,
But being both from me, both to each friend,
I guess one angel in another's hell.   12
    Yet this shall I ne'er know, but live in doubt,
    Till my bad angel fire my good one out.

Sonnet 144 makes the love-triangle emotionally explicit: to Shakespeare, the young man is a source of comfort, and the dark lady a source of despair. Like the good and bad angels in medieval mystery plays, they continually counsel and tempt him ('suggest me still').

Shakespeare suspects that the dark lady has corrupted the young man, stealing his love. Lines 12–14 may simply express the hope that she will reject the young man, but they also contain strong sexual implications, namely that she may have infected him with a sexually transmitted disease. In Elizabethan slang, 'hell' implied the female sexual organ, and 'fire out' meant to give someone a sexually transmitted disease.

The sonnet is an intense reflection on the theme addressed in a lighter vein in Sonnet 143. Compare the two sonnets, thinking particularly of their imagery and of how you respond to their poetic effect. You may also find it valuable to make comparisons with Sonnets 40–42.

---

coloured ill dark-complexioned, dark-haired
foul pride ugly appearance
directly completely, truly

both from me, both to each friend absent from me, and friendly with each other

145

Those lips that Love's own hand did make
Breathed forth the sound that said 'I hate'
To me that languished for her sake;
But when she saw my woeful state,   4
Straight in her heart did mercy come,
Chiding that tongue that ever sweet
Was used in giving gentle doom,
And taught it thus anew to greet: 8
'I hate' she altered with an end
That followed it as gentle day
Doth follow night, who like a fiend
From heaven to hell is flown away: 12
    'I hate' from hate away she threw,
    And saved my life, saying 'not you'.

Sonnet 145 is different from all the other sonnets. It is written in tetrameters or lines of four stresses, rather than the familiar pentameters or lines of five stresses. Its meaning seems unambiguous: out of pity for Shakespeare, the lady changed 'I hate' into 'I hate not you'.

Critics are divided about the sonnet's poetic quality. Some think it was not written by Shakespeare and is very trivial. Others are confident that it is by Shakespeare, and point out that its vocabulary echoes that of Sonnet 144 ('fiend', 'heaven', 'hell'). They argue that it is appropriately placed in the sequence.

Still others think it is 'juvenilia', a poem written when Shakespeare was very young. They suggest that 'hate away' in line 13 may be a pun on the name of Shakespeare's wife, Anne Hathaway, and that line 14 could be spoken as 'Anne saved my life'.

What is your judgement of the sonnet's poetic quality?

Love's Venus's or Cupid's
languished pined, suffered
  depression

Straight immediately
Chiding scolding, rebuking
gentle doom kind judgement

146

Poor soul, the centre of my sinful earth,
[...] these rebel pow'rs that thee array,
Why dost thou pine within and suffer dearth
Painting thy outward walls so costly gay?   4
Why so large cost, having so short a lease,
Dost thou upon thy fading mansion spend?
Shall worms, inheritors of this excess,
Eat up thy charge? Is this thy body's end?   8
Then, soul, live thou upon thy servant's loss,
And let that pine to aggravate thy store;
Buy terms divine in selling hours of dross;
Within be fed, without be rich no more: 12
   So shalt thou feed on Death, that feeds on men,
   And Death once dead, there's no more dying then.

Sonnet 146 is often claimed to be Shakespeare's only Christian sonnet. It reflects on the brevity of human life, 'so short a lease', and on the need to gain eternal life by preferring the life of the spirit or 'soul' over the pleasures of the body.

The body is portrayed in uncomplimentary images: 'sinful earth', 'outward walls', 'fading mansion', 'servant'. Similar negative metaphors describe how the passions indulge in extravagant display: 'rebel pow'rs', 'costly gay', 'excess', 'charge', 'dross' (garbage).

The sonnet questions why the soul experiences sorrow and loss, whilst the body dresses and behaves with extravagant show. It claims that triumph over death will be achieved through the denial of the body.

No one knows what Shakespeare intended as the first two syllables of line 2. Many suggestions have been made, including 'Prey to', 'Vexed by', 'Hiding', 'Throne of', 'Ruled by' and 'Slave of'. Make your own suggestion appropriate to the sense, mood and images of the sonnet.

rebel pow'rs body and passions
array dress, decorate
pine within grieve inwardly, waste away
dearth famine, want

costly gay expensively flashy
charge expensive adornments, body
aggravate increase
store resources
terms divine everlasting life

My love is as a fever, longing still
For that which longer nurseth the disease,
Feeding on that which doth preserve the ill,
Th'uncertain sickly appetite to please.   4
My reason, the physician to my love,
Angry that his prescriptions are not kept,
Hath left me, and I desperate now approve
Desire is death, which physic did except.   8
Past cure I am, now reason is past care,
And, frantic mad with evermore unrest,
My thoughts and my discourse as madmen's are,
At random from the truth vainly expressed: 12
    For I have sworn thee fair, and thought thee bright,
    Who art as black as hell, as dark as night.

This sonnet develops the image of love as a disease. It begins with a simile, 'My love is as a fever', and continues to explore the comparison: love longs for that which makes it ill; love will not obey reason; love ignores rational advice; love is beyond all cure. As a result, reason stops caring ('is past care'), and the poet is left in a state of raving madness, speaking untruths.

Lines 13–14 express the untruth which Shakespeare once believed, and which is the source of his 'disease'. He once thought the dark lady to be 'fair' and 'bright', but, in reality, she is physically and morally corrupt.

Find all the words in lines 1–12 which help to create the image of love as a disease.

longing still always desiring
longer nurseth prolongs and
  nourishes
uncertain unpredictable
kept followed
approve find, prove

physic did except medicine
  prevented
evermore unrest continual
  uneasiness
discourse talk
At random far from, different
vainly expressed foolishly spoken

148

O me! what eyes hath love put in my head,
Which have no correspondence with true sight?
Or, if they have, where is my judgement fled,
That censures falsely what they see aright? 4
If that be fair whereon my false eyes dote,
What means the world to say it is not so?
If it be not, then love doth well denote
Love's eye is not so true as all men's: no, 8
How can it? O how can love's eye be true,
That is so vexed with watching and with tears?
No marvel then though I mistake my view:
The sun itself sees not till heaven clears. 12
   O cunning love, with tears thou keep'st me blind,
   Lest eyes, well seeing, thy foul faults should find.

Sonnet 148 echoes the subject of Sonnets 113, 114 and 137, the power of love to distort perception. In pairs of lines, it repeatedly expresses puzzlement. Love makes eyes see wrongly, it makes judgement err, and sees beauty in what other people ('the world') judge ugly. Lines 9–14 seem to resolve the puzzlement. Shakespeare's eyes are so troubled by sleeplessness and tears that he cannot see the physical and moral imperfections of the dark lady.

The word 'love' occurs five times in the sonnet. It could refer to Cupid, to the dark lady, or to the emotion of love. Try to keep all three possibilities in mind as you read. Do you think it is preferable to narrow the meaning to only one possibility in some lines?

The sonnet structure could be thought of as seven couplets. If the sonnet were read aloud, do you think that there should be a distinct pause after each pair of lines?

correspondence agreement
judgement reason
censures falsely judges wrongly
dote love passionately

denote signify, show
vexed troubled, clouded
watching sleeplessness
mistake my view see wrongly

149

Canst thou, O cruel, say I love thee not,
When I against myself with thee partake?
Do I not think on thee when I forgot
Am of myself, all tyrant for thy sake? 4
Who hateth thee that I do call my friend?
On whom frown'st thou that I do fawn upon?
Nay, if thou lour'st on me, do I not spend
Revenge upon myself with present moan? 8
What merit do I in myself respect
That is so proud thy service to despise,
When all my best doth worship thy defect,
Commanded by the motion of thine eyes? 12
    But, love, hate on, for now I know thy mind:
    Those that can see thou lov'st, and I am blind.

Sonnet 149 seems to be a response to the dark lady's complaint that Shakespeare does not love her. How can you say that, he replies, when I side with you against myself, treat myself harshly for your sake, reject your enemies and refuse to flatter them, and immediately grieve if you even frown on me? Lines 9–12 condemn any quality of his which refuses to serve her. All his good qualities worship her faults. A mere glance from her ('the motion of thine eyes') has power over him.

Lines 13–14 are open to a range of interpretations, for example:

a 'But let my love continue to hate what you hate. Because I know you love those who admire you, and being blind to your faults, I admire you most.'

b 'But keep on hating me, I know you love those who see your faults. My blindness to those faults is proof of my love.'

Do you find one of the above interpretations more convincing than the other? If you feel dissatisfied with both, suggest your own.

---

with thee partake take your side, unite
forgot ... tyrant forget and punish myself

fawn upon flatter and cringe to
lour'st frown, scowl
present moan instant suffering
defect faults

O from what pow'r hast thou this pow'rful might
With insufficiency my heart to sway,
To make me give the lie to my true sight,
And swear that brightness doth not grace the day? 4
Whence hast thou this becoming of things ill,
That in the very refuse of thy deeds
There is such strength and warrantise of skill
That in my mind thy worst all best exceeds? 8
Who taught thee how to make me love thee more,
The more I hear and see just cause of hate?
O, though I love what others do abhor,
With others thou shouldst not abhor my state. 12
    If thy unworthiness raised love in me,
    More worthy I to be beloved of thee.

Shakespeare continues to question why he loves the dark lady in spite of her all too evident faults. Where does she gain the power to make her defects command his love? What makes him see distortedly, even swearing that the sun doesn't shine by day? How is it that she can make bad things appear good, and make even her most loathsome actions seem excellent? Why is it that the more Shakespeare sees reasons to detest her, the more he loves her?

In lines 11–14, Shakespeare pleads with the dark lady not to hate him. His love of her faults deserves love in return.

Sonnets 149–50 are sometimes claimed to be psychologically accurate, showing how some lovers feel. Such people are rejected and despised by the person they love, and they are aware that their lover is unattractive and immoral. Yet, in spite of such rejection and defects, their love grows stronger. Do you find this portrayal convincing?

---

pow'r power, god, supernatural source
insufficiency defects
sway rule
give the lie to call a liar
grace make beautiful

becoming of things ill power to make bad seem good
refuse worst elements
warrantise of skill authority, appeal
state condition (of loving you)

151

Love is too young to know what conscience is,
Yet who knows not conscience is born of love?
Then, gentle cheater, urge not my amiss,
Lest guilty of my faults thy sweet self prove.   4
For thou betraying me, I do betray
My nobler part to my gross body's treason:
My soul doth tell my body that he may
Triumph in love; flesh stays no farther reason,   8
But rising at thy name doth point out thee
As his triumphant prize. Proud of this pride,
He is contented thy poor drudge to be,
To stand in thy affairs, fall by thy side.   12
    No want of conscience hold it that I call
    Her 'love' for whose dear love I rise and fall.

Sonnet 151 warns the dark lady not to rebuke Shakespeare's faults, in case she is shown to be similarly sinful. His sin is that his bodily desire ignores what his conscience tells him. Sex triumphs over reason, and he becomes sexually aroused at the mere sound of her name.

Lines 8–14 are full of words signifying male sexual desire: 'flesh', 'rising', 'point', 'Proud', 'stand', 'fall', 'rise and fall'. Even the word 'conscience' had a sexual meaning in Shakespeare's time (as well as the usual meaning of knowledge of good and bad).

The sonnet has been a source of great embarrassment to many readers, who feel uncomfortable about its explicit sexual references. Some have called it obscene, and refused to believe that Shakespeare wrote it. Imagine that you are a teacher. You are going to invite your class to discuss Sonnet 151. How will you go about it?

---

conscience morality
cheater betrayer
urge not my amiss don't stress my sin
thy sweet self prove you also accuse yourself
nobler part soul, reason

gross body's treason sexual desire
flesh stays no farther reason sexual desire cannot wait
drudge servant
stand in thy affairs serve you (in business and sexually)

152

In loving thee thou know'st I am forsworn,
But thou art twice forsworn to me love swearing:
In act thy bed-vow broke, and new faith torn
In vowing new hate after new love bearing.   4
But why of two oaths' breach do I accuse thee,
When I break twenty? I am perjured most,
For all my vows are oaths but to misuse thee,
And all my honest faith in thee is lost.   8
For I have sworn deep oaths of thy deep kindness,
Oaths of thy love, thy truth, thy constancy,
And to enlighten thee gave eyes to blindness,
Or made them swear against the thing they see: 12
    For I have sworn thee fair: more perjured eye,
    To swear against the truth so foul a lie.

This sonnet contains at least seventeen references to promise-keeping or promise-breaking. It presents intriguing puzzles about who is involved. Does line 1 refer to Shakespeare's broken faith with the young man, or with his wife Anne Hathaway? Was the broken 'bed-vow' in line 3 made to the dark lady's husband, to Shakespeare, or to another man? Does 'new love' in line 4 imply a reconciliation with Shakespeare, or is it the dark lady's love for the young man?

However, these puzzles are probably far less significant than the emotions in lines 5–14. Shakespeare accuses himself of breaking many vows. He has sworn that the dark lady is kind, loving, truthful, faithful and beautiful, but all the evidence of his eyes tells him that such claims are lies. His integrity has gone (line 8), his 'eye' is perjured.

How important is it to know who's who in this sonnet and in the whole sonnet sequence? You will find help with this question of the biographical background of *The Sonnets* on pages 146–8.

---

am forsworn have broken my vow, am false
bed-vow marriage vows
new love bearing loving someone new
breach breaking

perjured false
misuse deceive, tell lies about
truth honesty
constancy faithfulness
enlighten thee make you appear beautiful

153

Cupid laid by his brand and fell asleep:
A maid of Dian's this advantage found,
And his love-kindling fire did quickly steep
In a cold valley-fountain of that ground;   4
Which borrowed from this holy fire of Love
A dateless lively heat, still to endure,
And grew a seething bath, which yet men prove
Against strange maladies a sovereign cure.   8
But at my mistress' eye Love's brand new fired,
The boy for trial needs would touch my breast;
I, sick withal, the help of bath desired,
And thither hied, a sad distempered guest;   12
    But found no cure: the bath for my help lies
    Where Cupid got new fire – my mistress' eyes.

Sonnets 153 and 154 are variations of the following story, which can be traced back in poetry for over a thousand years before Shakespeare's time:

> Cupid, god of love, lays down his flaming torch of love ('brand'), and sleeps. A maid of Diana, goddess of chastity, seizes her chance and steals the torch. She extinguishes it in a nearby stream. But the torch inflames the water, making it foaming hot ('seething'). The hot spring then becomes a cure for all kinds of illnesses.

Lines 9–14 add Shakespeare's contribution to the story. The dark lady's eye relights Cupid's torch, making Shakespeare fall in love with her. He seeks a cure, but the hot waters fail him. His only comfort is love from her eyes. A sombre interpretation is possible if you recall that, in Elizabethan times, people believed that steaming in a hot tub of water was a cure for sexually transmitted diseases.

---

advantage opportunity
steep extinguish
of that ground nearby
dateless lively eternally living
still to endure always lasting
prove take, find to be

strange maladies extreme illnesses
  (sexually transmitted diseases)
The boy Cupid
for trial to try it out
hied hastened
distempered sick

The little Love-god lying once asleep
Laid by his side his heart-inflaming brand,
Whilst many nymphs that vowed chaste life to keep
Came tripping by; but in her maiden hand   4
The fairest votary took up that fire
Which many legions of true hearts had warmed,
And so the general of hot desire
Was sleeping by a virgin hand disarmed.   8
This brand she quenchèd in a cool well by,
Which from Love's fire took heat perpetual,
Growing a bath and healthful remedy
For men diseased; but I, my mistress' thrall,   12
    Came there for cure, and this by that I prove:
    Love's fire heats water, water cools not love.

In lines 1–12, Sonnet 154 tells the same story as the previous sonnet. Once again, Shakespeare finds no cure for his enslavement to the dark lady. The metaphor in line 14 implies that, although love can inflame the coldest of hearts (which seem like an icy stream), no water can cure the fever of love.

Some people believe that Sonnets 153–4 refer to a visit Shakespeare made to the city of Bath, which even in Elizabethan times had a reputation for the medicinal value of its hot water springs. Others find this suggestion highly improbable.

A more important question about the two sonnets is how appropriate they are as an *envoi* (a conclusion to a sonnet sequence), representing the poet's final thoughts. How fitting a conclusion to the whole sonnet sequence do you judge them to be? Consider their style, theme, imagery, 'story' and closing couplets.

---

nymphs maids
chaste life chastity
tripping dancing
votary worshipper, someone who
  has taken a vow (of chastity)

legions multitudes, armies
general leader (Cupid)
quenchèd extinguished
Growing becoming
thrall slave

The sonnet tradition

Well over two hundred years before Shakespeare was born, an Italian poet living in Avignon in the South of France caught sight of a woman who was to inspire some of the most famous love poetry of all time. The poet was Francesco Petrarca, known as Petrarch (1304–74). He called the woman Laura, but her real identity is not known.

Long after Laura's death, Petrarch collected together the poems he had written to her and about her. His *Rime* (or *Canzoniere*) enjoyed huge popularity. It began a tradition in which the fourteen-line sonnet was used to declare unwavering devotion to a beautiful but cold and disdainful lady. With great lyrical intensity, each sonnet told of the poet's suffering as the unattainable woman cruelly and implacably refused his advances. Sonnets expressed the poetry of frustration, of unrequited love.

Although sonnets flourished in Italy and France, they were only slowly taken up by English poets. For example, Geoffrey Chaucer (1345–1400) included a translation of one of Petrarch's sonnets in his *Troilus and Criseyde*, but it was only much later that Sir Thomas Wyatt and the Earl of Surrey made the sonnet form familiar to English readers.

Sir Thomas Wyatt (1503–42) travelled widely in Europe as a diplomat. He translated many of Petrarch's sonnets into English. In his own sonnets, Wyatt added a new 'anti-Petrarchan' theme: the desire of the lover to break free of the love which enslaves him. It was a theme that Shakespeare would imaginatively extend.

Henry Howard, Earl of Surrey (1517–47) made two unique contributions to sonnet writing through his development of Petrarch's sonnets. He established the rhyme scheme that was to become the 'English' or 'Shakespearean' sonnet (ABAB CDCD EFEF GG). He also added a new theme: male friendship. As well as expressing love for an unattainable lady, Surrey wrote admiring sonnets about male friends. Both of Surrey's innovations were to be central to Shakespeare's sonnets.

The poems of Wyatt and Surrey were published in 1557 in *Songs and Sonnets* (better known as *Tottel's Miscellany*). The publication seemed to have little immediate impact, and very few sonnets were written in the following thirty years. In the 1590s, however, there was an explosion of sonnet writing in England. It became the most fashionable literary activity of all, and poets took an almost obsessive delight in word-play.

Sir Thomas Wyatt was all-too familiar with the hazards of love. He was imprisoned in the Tower of London by Henry VIII, on suspicion of being one of Anne Boleyn's lovers.

Like Wyatt, Henry Howard, the Earl of Surrey, was a man of action as well as a poet. He fought against the enemies of Henry VIII in Scotland and France, and was wounded in battle. He fell out of favour several times during Henry's reign, and was eventually imprisoned in the Tower of London. On the strength of damning evidence given by his own sister, he was later executed on Tower Hill for treason.

In 1591, Sir Philip Sidney's sonnet sequence *Astrophil and Stella* was published. It sparked off a brief but glitteringly intense and fruitful period, when writing and reading sonnets became a vogue among the educated classes. For example, Edmund Spenser's sonnet sequence *Amoretti* was published in 1595.

Astrophil and Stella is a sequence of 108 sonnets and eleven songs. Astrophil ('lover of a star') loves Stella ('star'), but his love is hopeless. All he achieves is a kiss, snatched whilst Stella is asleep. It seems probable that the sonnets were based on a real-life romance, with Sidney (Astrophil) in love with Penelope Devereux (Stella), who later married Lord Rich.

Sir Philip Sidney (1554–86) was born at Penshurst Place in Kent, into a high-ranking aristocratic family. He travelled widely in Europe on diplomatic business. He studied constantly on his travels, deepening his knowledge of literature, music, ethics, history and other subjects. He died a hero's death (see opposite), aged only thirty-one. After his death, his reputation grew, and he became enshrined in history as the perfect English example of Renaissance man: courtier, poet, soldier, statesman and critic.

The legend which grew out of the heroic manner of Sidney's death contributed to the wildly enthusiastic reception that greeted the publication of his sonnet sequence in 1591. It began not just a fashion, but a craze for sonnets which lasted for a decade, before vanishing as abruptly as it had begun.

Everyone who considered himself a poet (at that time nearly all poetry was written by men) tried his hand at sonnets. All took Sidney's sonnets as their model, pouring out loving verses addressed to a cold, disdainful lady. Today, most of these poets have been completely forgotten, but in London in the 1590s, their sonnet sequences were the talk of the town. Like the knights of medieval times who jousted with each other, governed by a strict code of chivalry, the sonneteers of late Elizabethan England competed for critical attention as they modelled their verses on Sidney, Petrarch, and the French and Italian sonnets.

It was in this fertile atmosphere that Shakespeare's sonnets were conceived. Just as Shakespeare had learned much about play-writing from the work of other playwrights, so the sonnets of Sidney and the playfulness in language of all the sonneteers of the 1590s must have fuelled his imagination. The time for writing sonnets was ripe, and Shakespeare's poetic genius responded with astonishing fruitfulness to the opportunity that was so briefly available.

In 1585, Sir Philip Sidney was appointed as governor of Flushing in the Low Countries (Holland). He was fatally wounded at Zutphen, a small town near Arnhem. It was said that, as he was carried away from the field of battle, Sidney gave his water-bottle to a dying soldier, saying 'Thy necessity is yet greater than mine'. He was given a magnificent state funeral in St Paul's Cathedral.

The sonnet vogue of the 1590s was accompanied by a fashion in painting which gave men a distinctively 'poetic' appearance.

Themes: love, time and poetry

One answer to the question 'What are the sonnets about?' is that they tell the story of Shakespeare's troubled relationships with two deeply flawed lovers. Both the young man of Sonnets 1–126 and the dark lady of Sonnets 127–54 cause Shakespeare great anguish as they betray his love and trust (see page 3 for a summary of the 'story').

Another way of answering the question is to identify the major themes which *The Sonnets* explore in many different ways: love, time and poetry.

Love

> Two loves I have, of comfort and despair.
>
> Sonnet 144

Like all other sonnet sequences of Elizabethan times, Shakespeare's sonnets are very obviously about love. But no other poet explored the nature of love so perceptively and so variously. The feelings expressed for the young man and the dark lady range from unqualified devotion, through anxious jealousy and suspicion, to intense cynical criticism. The poet's emotions touch the extremes of joy and sorrow, of tender love and acute self-loathing, as Shakespeare writes about both idealistic love and blind sexual lust.

Sonnets 1–126 show that every experience provokes thoughts of the young man. Some sonnets (97, 98 and 113) arise from the pain of separation, real or imagined:

> How like a winter hath my absence been
> From thee, the pleasure of the fleeting year!
>
> Sonnet 97

Love so pervades the weary journeys of Sonnets 27 and 28 that night brings no rest, only sleeplessness and the anguish of absence:

> But day doth daily draw my sorrows longer,
> And night doth nightly make griefs' length seem stronger.
>
> Sonnet 28

Yet love also brings anxiety and jealousy, together with the torturing fear of losing the young man:

> For thee watch I, whilst thou dost wake elsewhere,
> From me far off, with others all too near.
>
> Sonnet 61

In Sonnet 147, love for the dark lady is felt as a sickness ('My love is as a fever'), making the poet 'past cure' and 'frantic mad'. In marked contrast, in Sonnets 25, 29, 30, 31, and 37, love becomes a source of comfort. For example, Sonnet 30 tells of grief and sadness, but concludes with great reassurance:

> But if the while I think on thee (dear friend)
> All losses are restored, and sorrows end.

Love is a compensation for the poet's own lack of status or success, as recorded in Sonnet 29 ('When in disgrace with Fortune and men's eyes'):

> Haply I think on thee, and then my state
> (Like to the lark at break of day arising
> From sullen earth) sings hymns at heaven's gate.

The love theme of *The Sonnets* becomes ever more interwoven with a concern which runs through all of Shakespeare's plays, namely false appearance. The young man may be outwardly beautiful, but *The Sonnets* record growing suspicion that, inwardly, he is corrupt. His morality and judgement are undermined by his sensuality and his liking for flattery. Appearance does not match reality. Sonnet 69 expresses the criticism directly:

> But why thy odour matcheth not thy show,
> The soil is this, that thou dost common grow.

The Sonnets chronicle Shakespeare's growing realisation that the young man's affections stray elsewhere. The ideal love which can be enjoyed in dreams vanishes in the cold light of day:

> Thus have I had thee as a dream doth flatter,
> In sleep a king, but waking no such matter.
>   Sonnet 87

In Sonnet 94, the distrust is expressed in a compelling image:

> Lilies that fester smell far worse than weeds.

Such suspicion of the young man's inconstancy, of his unfaithfulness, stands in stark contrast to the definition of love given in Sonnet 116:

>   love is not love
> Which alters when it alteration finds,
> Or bends with the remover to remove.
> O no, it is an ever-fixèd mark
> That looks on tempests and is never shaken.

Time (and immortality through children and poetry)

Throughout Sonnets 1–126, Time and its destructive power cruelly threaten youth and beauty. Everything will fade and die as Time moves on remorselessly, changing everything:

> But reckoning Time, whose millioned accidents
> Creep in 'twixt vows, and change decrees of kings,
> Tan sacred beauty, blunt the sharp'st intents,
> Divert strong minds to th'course of alt'ring things
>
> Sonnet 115

Time is like a character in the drama of *The Sonnets*. It is personified in a multitude of ways: 'this bloody tyrant Time', 'Devouring Time', 'swift-footed Time' and 'never-resting time'. Its 'cruel hand' and 'thievish progress' have no pity as it steals beauty. Sonnet 2 sees Time as a besieging army which will wreak havoc on youthful loveliness:

> When forty winters shall besiege thy brow,
> And dig deep trenches in thy beauty's field.

Nothing seems able to withstand the destructive power of Time's 'fell hand', which sweeps everything away to death. Just as human life is subject to mortality ('Time will come and take my love away'), so Time exercises its dominion over all things:

> Since brass, nor stone, nor earth, nor boundless sea,
> But sad mortality o'ersways their power.
>
> Sonnet 65

> Like as the waves make towards the pebbled shore,
> So do our minutes hasten to their end.
>
> Sonnet 60

Most poets before Shakespeare accepted the inevitability of Time's decay of human life. Their response was to urge the pursuit of pleasure, and the enjoyment of the present moment. Their theme was *carpe diem* or 'seize the day'. The poet Robert Herrick expressed it as 'Gather ye rosebuds while ye may'; in the popular proverb, it becomes 'Eat, drink and be merry, for tomorrow we die'.

Shakespeare takes a quite different stance in *The Sonnets*, and the theme of *carpe diem* does not appear. In contrast, *The Sonnets* can be read as a defiant challenge to the ravages of Time, a refusal to accept the inevitability of 'his scythe and crooked knife'. Time, the enemy, can be defied and defeated. Love itself can conquer Time: 'Love's not Time's fool'. Youth and beauty can live on eternally. Children and Shakespeare's verse will ensure immortality for the loved one.

Sonnets 1–17 urge the young man to 'make war upon this bloody tyrant Time' by marrying and having children. His children will ensure that his youth and beauty live on, because children ('breed') are the only guarantee against Time's wasteful devastation:

> And nothing 'gainst Time's scythe can make defence
> Save breed to brave him when he takes thee hence.
>
> Sonnet 12

After Sonnet 17, the theme of achieving immortality by having children is abandoned, and Shakespeare mounts an even more confident challenge to Time. The idea that verse can transcend Time's hostility is boldly asserted in Sonnet 18:

> Nor shall Death brag thou wand'rest in his shade,
> When in eternal lines to time thou grow'st.
>> So long as men can breathe or eyes can see,
>> So long lives this, and this gives life to thee.

Verse will last longer than any memorial:

> Not marble nor the gilded monuments
> Of princes shall outlive this pow'rful rhyme.
>
> Sonnet 55

Although 'Time doth transfix the flourish set on youth', poetry will overcome Time's tyranny. Again and again *The Sonnets* assert that Time's destructiveness can be conquered by poetry itself:

> Yet do thy worst, old Time: despite thy wrong,
> My love shall in my verse ever live young.
>
> Sonnet 19

> And yet to times in hope my verse shall stand,
> Praising thy worth, despite his cruel hand.
>
> Sonnet 60

In Sonnet 100, Shakespeare calls on his Muse to 'make Time's spoils despisèd every where'. He ends Sonnet 107 with a triumphant claim of his poetry's victory over death itself:

> My love looks fresh, and Death to me subscribes,
> Since spite of him I'll live in this poor rhyme,
>
> ...
>
>> And thou in this shalt find thy monument,
>> When tyrants' crests and tombs of brass are spent.

Poetry

Shakespeare's confidence that verse can transcend and conquer the destructiveness of Time is only one aspect of his fascination with the nature of poetry and the craft of writing verse. He sometimes criticises his own ability as a poet, speaking in Sonnet 16 of his 'pupil pen', and in Sonnet 85 of his 'tongue-tied Muse'. Elsewhere, Shakespeare questions why he continues to write only sonnets, rather than some other kind of verse:

> Why is my verse so barren of new pride?
> So far from variation or quick change?
>
> Sonnet 76

Working within the sonnet tradition (see pages 178–81), Shakespeare draws upon its resources, but also challenges and extends it. This challenge (his 'anti-Petrarchan theme') has three notable elements: the young man, the dark lady, and the use of metaphor.

Petrarch, and the many sonneteers who followed his example, addressed their poems to a beautiful but unattainable woman. Shakespeare dramatically changed that convention, addressing the bulk of his sonnets not to a woman, but to a young man.

Shakespeare's second departure from tradition lies in the way in which he depicts his mistress. She is far from being the conventional Elizabethan ideal of fair-haired virtuous beauty, or the 'perfect' women praised by earlier poets. In the sharpest contrast, she is 'a woman coloured ill', all too available to other men. She is 'the bay where all men ride', a woman whose sexual appetite corrupts the young man and makes her false. Two couplets record Shakespeare's changed perception of the dark lady, and express his revulsion:

> For I have sworn thee fair, and thought thee bright,
> Who art as black as hell, as dark as night.
>
> Sonnet 147

> For I have sworn thee fair: more perjured eye,
> To swear against the truth so foul a lie.
>
> Sonnet 152

The third way in which Shakespeare moves away from the Petrarchan tradition is in his handling of metaphor. Like other Elizabethan sonnet sequences, Shakespeare's sonnets celebrate the beauty of the beloved in seemingly extravagant comparisons. Many praise the beauty of the young man as exceeding all other perfect things:

> Shall I compare thee to a summer's day?
> Thou art more lovely and more temperate.
>
> Sonnet 18

But other sonnets are deeply suspicious of such exaggerated comparisons. Shakespeare criticises the poets who falsely compare their ladies' beauty with all that is lovely in nature:

> Making a couplement of proud compare
> With sun and moon, with earth and sea's rich gems,
> With April's first-born flowers, and all things rare.
>
> Sonnet 21

The sonnet continues with a direct rejection of such extravagant comparisons:

> O, let me, true in love, but truly write,
> And then believe me, my love is as fair
> As any mother's child, though not so bright
> As those gold candles fixed in heaven's air.

This modesty and the rejection of hyperbolic comparisons is reflected in those sonnets which settle for praise expressed in the simplest language. For example, Sonnet 84 clearly states where truth and sincerity are to be found in poetry:

> Who is it that says most which can say more
> Than this rich praise – that you alone are you,
> …
> But he that writes of you, if he can tell
> That you are you, so dignifies his story.

The depiction of the dark lady is bitingly honest, declaring that she is not conventionally beautiful, and that comparisons like those of Sonnet 21 ('With sun and moon, with earth and sea's rich gems') are false. In Sonnet 130, Shakespeare mocks such over-the-top comparisons:

> My mistress' eyes are nothing like the sun;
> Coral is far more red than her lips' red.

The same sonnet arrives at a similar conclusion to Sonnet 21, rejecting the exaggeration of traditional poetic metaphors:

> And yet, by heaven, I think my love as rare
> As any she belied with false compare.

The following section on the language of *The Sonnets* also bears witness to Shakespeare's fascination with the craft of writing verse.

The language of *The Sonnets*

Dramatic language

Very obviously, a poem is different from a play. *The Sonnets* are not dramatic in the same way that *Hamlet* and *Macbeth* are dramatic. There is no 'action' or dialogue. Nonetheless, *The Sonnets* are intensely dramatic in their subject, themes and images. The cast list is small (a poet, a young man, a woman, a rival poet), but its members are like characters in a play, caught up in the conflicts of divided emotions.

Other 'characters' play their parts: time, death, love and poetry itself. As personifications, they enact their own drama. For example, 'never-resting time' defeats the loveliness of summer (Sonnet 5), 'wasteful Time' conspires with Decay (Sonnet 15), and 'that churl Death' covers the poet's bones with dust (Sonnet 32).

As Shakespeare reflects on the perplexities of love, his language expresses the same restless, dynamic qualities as the language of his plays. In what seem like soliloquies or monologues, *The Sonnets* attempt to persuade: they plead, implore, warn, reason, chide, threaten, argue, flatter and assert. The language conveys the way in which Shakespeare struggles with his feelings in the face of the real or imagined difficulties of his relationships.

Like the voices of the characters in his plays, the voice of Shakespeare's sonnets explores the widest range of feeling. It is in turn lyrical, joyous, passionate, anguished, defiant, sensuous, meditative and self-questioning, ironic and sincere.

One of Shakespeare's favourite language devices is *antithesis*, the opposition of words or phrases against each other. He uses it in every sonnet and in each one of his plays. As a playwright, Shakespeare knew that conflict lies at the heart of all drama. His writing embodies that conflict in its use of antithesis. Just as person is set against person in the plays (Hamlet against Claudius, Lear against his daughters), so Shakespeare sets word against word in *The Sonnets*.

Such oppositions heighten the intensity of feeling in *The Sonnets*. For example, Sonnet 144 is full of antitheses, as Shakespeare reflects on his love for two persons:

Two loves I have, of comfort and despair.

The balancing or contrasting of words and phrases produces sharp and striking effects as words oppose each other. In Sonnet 12, a single line contains a double antithesis as 'day' contrasts with 'night', and 'brave' opposes 'hideous':

And see the brave day sunk in hideous night.

Imagery

The Sonnets are rich in imagery: emotionally charged words and phrases which conjure up vivid mental pictures in the imagination. Imagery increases emotional appeal through memorable comparisons. It carries powerful significance, using striking metaphors or similes for ideas or feelings, as in Sonnet 55: 'unswept stone, besmeared with sluttish time' (metaphor), and Sonnet 97: 'How like a winter hath my absence been' (simile).

Shakespeare's poetic and dramatic imagination responded both to what he read and to what he saw around him. For instance, the city of London and the everyday world of Elizabethan England provide Shakespeare with an abundant source of images. Commerce and wealth, the law, music, alchemy, astrology, painting, perfume and medicine occur frequently throughout *The Sonnets*.

Shakespeare's dislike of cosmetics, and his ambivalent feelings about his own profession as an actor and playwright also provide imagery. So, too, do the great memorials in stone or brass which Shakespeare saw as he travelled around the country. They are often called upon to illustrate the theme of time's destructive power, as in Sonnet 107:

When tyrants' crests and tombs of brass are spent.

The imagery of nature (the seasons, flowers, birds, the sun) predominates. The countryside of Shakespeare's youth enriches many sonnets with sustained comparisons or striking lines. For example:

(Like to the lark at break of day arising
From sullen earth) sings hymns at heaven's gate
                    Sonnet 29

proud-pied April (dressed in all his trim)
                    Sonnet 98

The sea and navigation provide imagery to suggest the rival poet's power or the ever constant nature of true love:

Was it the proud full sail of his great verse
                    Sonnet 86

It is the star to every wand'ring bark
Sonnet 116

The human body supplies another rich source of imagery, notably the heart and eye. In Sonnet 46, imagery of the body and of war reflect the conflicts of love in an elaborate conceit (comparison):

Mine eye and heart are at a mortal war.

Sometimes a sonnet will contain a single image which pervades the whole poem. For example, Sonnet 33 is a sustained comparison between the sun obscured by clouds and Shakespeare's feelings when the young man proves fickle in love. Other sonnets contain a number of images. Lines 1–8 of Sonnet 12 picture a clock, a sunset, faded flowers, white hair, bare trees in winter, sheltering cattle and harvested corn.

Ambiguity

All poets relish ambiguity: the power of language to evoke different responses because a word or phrase has more than one meaning. Such ambiguity can increase the pleasure of a reader of poetry. An obvious example is in Sonnet 138:

Therefore I lie with her, and she with me.

Here, 'lie with' can mean both 'tell untruths to' and 'sleep with'. The double meaning heightens enjoyment as interpretation wavers between both possibilities, recognising both as valid.

Ambiguity is at the heart of poetry. Other uses of language seek to make meaning as clear and unambiguous as possible. In contrast, poetry revels in its power to evoke multiple responses, never settling on a single fixed meaning. Ambiguity celebrates the pleasures of doubt.

Other examples of ambiguous words include: 'love' (the emotion, the person who is loved, Cupid); 'dear' (expensive, the person loved) and 'fair' (just, beautiful, pale complexioned). If you turn to Sonnets 135 and 136, you will find at least nine possibilities for the meaning of 'will'!

Paradox and contradiction

Some sonnets revel in contradiction, expressing paradoxical statements which seem to be contrary to common sense. Sometimes the paradox is the subject of the sonnet itself, as in Sonnet 47 which suggests the way in which love overcomes the impossibility of being in two places at the same time:

Thyself, away, are present still with me.

Paradox in poetry matches the apparently absurd contradictions which love itself breeds. Paradox can be seen in the night and day imagery of Sonnet 43, which claims that eyes can see best in the dreams of dead night:

> When most I wink, then do mine eyes best see.

Shakespeare often expresses the paradox in the couplet at the end of a sonnet, contradicting the argument of the preceding twelve lines. For example, about thirty couplets begin with 'Yet' or 'But', showing that a challenge to the argument of lines 1–12 is about to follow. For example, in Sonnet 42, Shakespeare regrets that his friend and the dark lady have betrayed him and have become lovers. But he expresses comfort in the abrupt and paradoxical turn in the couplet:

> But here's the joy, my friend and I are one.
> Sweet flattery! then she loves but me alone.

Repetition

Poets frequently use repetition, because the internal patterns which it creates increase a poem's musicality and emotional appeal. The repetitions of rhythm and rhyme are obvious examples. Shakespeare sometimes weaves a pattern by repeating a word, such as 'will' in Sonnet 135 and 'all' in Sonnet 31.

Other forms of repetition are alliteration (words beginning with the same letter or sound) and assonance (the repetition of vowel sounds):

> When to the sessions of sweet silent thought.
> > Sonnet 30

> Since I left you, mine eye is in my mind.
> > Sonnet 113

A sonnet can contain all kinds of repetition. They may run throughout the whole sonnet, and may not be confined to either initial letter sounds or to a single line. In addition, there is repetition from sonnet to sonnet, as in the 'eye' / 'heart' of Sonnets 46 and 47.

Rhyme

Rhyme, or the repetition of sounds, helps to create pattern and symmetry, both of which add to the appeal of poetry. The rhyme scheme of *The Sonnets* is ABAB CDCD EFEF GG (see page 1). The rhymes are nearly always exact, with the exception of words whose pronunciation has changed since Shakespeare's time. A few examples of such changes are:

'love' / 'prove'	'deserts' / 'parts'
'die' / 'memory'	'haste' / 'past'
'word' / 'afford'	'dumb' / 'tomb'

Imagine that you have to give a public reading of some sonnets in which the pronunciation has changed (for example, Sonnets 17, 30 and 49). You have been invited to say a few words about pronunciation before your reading, and about whether or not you will rhyme these words. What will you say?

Pronouns

The Sonnets are intensely personal. Many are like meditations or self-questionings, as Shakespeare seems to be speaking to himself, exploring his feelings. Others are addressed directly to the young man or to the dark lady. It is not surprising, therefore, that personal pronouns and/or possessive adjectives appear so frequently: 'I', 'me', 'mine', 'you', 'thee', 'thy', and so on. Such words account for over fourteen per cent of all words in *The Sonnets* (that is, one word in every seven or eight is a personal pronoun and/or possessive adjective). Only Sonnet 129 is 'impersonal', without any such words.

Sonnet 134 contains 120 words, thirty-two of which are personal – over twenty-five per cent of the total. Read the sonnet aloud, emphasising each personal word, and identify each person referred to, for example, Shakespeare, the dark lady, the young man. (See also Sonnet 133.)

The couplet

The couplet (lines 13–14 of each sonnet) can be thought of as an epigram, a short witty climax which is often satirical or ironic. The couplet may reinforce and echo the preceding twelve lines, making a conclusion that clinches and confirms the argument. Alternatively, it may contradict the thought which has been developed in lines 1–12. Couplets which complete or carry on the thought of the first twelve lines often begin with 'Thus', 'So', 'Then' or 'Therefore' (for example, Sonnets 7, 25 and 87). The challenge to the previous thought may be a sharp sting in the tail, an ironic criticism, as in Sonnet 92:

> But what's so blessèd-fair that fears no blot?
> Thou mayst be false, and yet I know it not.

Monosyllables

Lines which contain only single-syllable words often convey feelings of great intensity. As you read *The Sonnets*, look out for examples which give the impression that the words are being emphatically hammered home:

Take all my loves, my love, yea, take them all.
                                                    Sonnet 40
All days are nights to see till I see thee,
All nights bright days when dreams do show thee me.
                                                    Sonnet 43
So long as men can breathe or eyes can see,
So long lives this, and this gives life to thee.
                                                    Sonnet 18

Mood

The mood or emotional tone of individual sonnets has been described in a variety of ways:

Lyrical Shall I compare thee to a summer's day? (Sonnet 18)
Anguished My love is as a fever, longing still (Sonnet 147)
Meditative Like as the waves make towards the pebbled shore (Sonnet 60)
Passionate Canst thou, O cruel, say I love thee not (Sonnet 149)
Enigmatic Was it the proud full sail of his great verse (Sonnet 86).

Choose a few sonnets for yourself and suggest their mood. Find several examples where the emotional tone changes within the sonnet.

Personification

Throughout *The Sonnets*, Shakespeare turns all kinds of things and abstractions into persons. For example, in Sonnet 28, day and night seem to take human form to oppress Shakespeare:

And each (though enemies to either's reign)
Do in consent shake hands to torture me.

You can find examples of the personification of time on page 184. Other examples include: Nature (Sonnets 4, 20, 67 and 68), Fortune (Sonnets 29, 37, 90, 111 and 124), Death (Sonnets 18, 32 and 107), War (Sonnet 55) and Love (Sonnet 145). In Sonnet 66, good and evil are personified dramatically:

And captive good attending captain ill.

Collect other examples of personification as you read, then design illustrations for those which appeal to you the most.

The development of the sonnet

The sonnet was a well-known and popular form of poetry for hundreds of years before Shakespeare (see page 178). Since his time, most major poets have tried their hand at sonnets. A few examples which you may wish to compare and contrast with Shakespeare's sonnets are:

John Donne *Death be not Proud*
John Milton *On his Blindness*
William Wordsworth *Composed upon Westminster Bridge*
Percy Bysshe Shelley *Ozymandias*
John Clare *First Sight of Spring*
John Keats *On First Looking into Chapman's Homer*
Elizabeth Barrett Browning *How do I love thee?*
Matthew Arnold *Shakespeare*
Christina Rossetti *Remember me*
Thomas Hardy *She, to Him*
Gerard Manley Hopkins *The Windhover*
Rupert Brooke *Sonnet Reversed*
Wilfred Owen *Anthem for Doomed Youth*
W. H. Auden *Who's Who*
Edna St Vincent Millay *Oh, Oh, you will be Sorry for that Word*
Philip Larkin *The Card-players*

Links with the plays

In *King Henry V*, the Dauphin claims that he once wrote a sonnet to his horse. In *Much Ado About Nothing*, Margaret jokes with Benedick:

MARGARET Will you then write me a sonnet in praise of my beauty?
BENEDICK In so high a style, Margaret, that no man living shall come over it.

Many of Shakespeare's plays echo the themes, imagery and language of *The Sonnets*. For example, *Troilus and Cressida* and *The Sonnets* share a common preoccupation with the destructive power of Time. The strongest parallels are found in the plays which Shakespeare wrote early in his career, although no one knows for certain when *The Sonnets* were written.

Some critics claim to find echoes of the dark lady of *The Sonnets* in Rosaline in *Love's Labour's Lost*. Both that play and *Romeo and Juliet* contain sonnets. *The Two Gentlemen of Verona* springs from the Romance Tradition of courtly love which also produced *The Sonnets*. The Tradition's themes of close male friendship, of the lover as servant, and of a complicated love triangle are echoed in *The Sonnets*. All three plays satirise a stock character of the sonnet tradition, namely the infatuated man hopelessly in love with an unattainable lady.

Every one of Shakespeare's plays contains the theme of appearance and reality. For example, Lady Macbeth urges Macbeth to 'Look like the innocent flower, but be the serpent under it'. Similarly, in *The Sonnets*, the beautiful appearance of the young man is contrasted with his moral corruption. In *Measure for Measure*, the corruption of the outwardly respectable and rational Angelo is mirrored in Sonnet 94: 'Lilies that fester smell far worse than weeds'.

Occasionally, theatre directors insert a sonnet into the play they are staging, because the sonnet can illuminate an aspect of the play. For instance, one production of *A Midsummer Night's Dream* used Sonnet 90 to heighten Hermia's sadness at losing her lover. Think about the play you are currently studying, and suggest a sonnet which could be included. Give the reasons why you think that the sonnet offers additional insight into the play.

Studying *The Sonnets*

Sometimes it is best to read a sonnet for enjoyment, as a private experience rather than as a topic for discussion. However, *The Sonnets* are often read in class, where group work can be fruitful, because you have opportunities to discuss your individual response to a sonnet with other students.

Whichever way you choose to study *The Sonnets*, remember that understanding and enjoyment are not mutually exclusive. They are both necessary parts of any informed response. But moving too quickly into detailed analysis can destroy enjoyment, so don't be afraid to experience the sonnet in free-wheeling exploration at first.

Each sonnet is rich in ambiguity, and because every reader's experience is different, any one sonnet will evoke a wide variety of responses. This edition encourages you to accept that a sonnet can have conflicting or paradoxical interpretations. You do not necessarily have to choose between different interpretations, but rather to see how each one could be valid. Answers to the question 'What is this sonnet about?' are usually best thought of as 'Both ... and ...', rather than as 'either ... or'.

It is often helpful to listen to a good reading of the sonnet before beginning a discussion. The sonnet can be read by the teacher or by a student. Volunteers only – never force anyone to read poetry aloud! Alternatively, good recordings are commercially available, for example on cassettes and CDs from Cambridge University Press.

After listening to the reading, work together in pairs or in small groups. Use the guidance provided on every sonnet page to help your discussion, but don't be afraid to follow your own interests as well, pursuing any questions about the sonnet which seem important to you. For example, the guidance often refers to Shakespeare as if the sonnet records an actual incident in his life, but you don't have to believe that. Indeed, it is often helpful to argue against such an interpretation.

What follows is a variety of suggestions from which you can choose those most suitable to your own needs and interests. As you study a sonnet, remember that Shakespeare delighted in playing with language. The practical activities aim at helping you to share that delight in word-play.

1 Helping discussion

You may prefer to have a discussion which is completely unstructured, although it is sometimes helpful to have some kind of framework to help you start off a discussion. Here is one such framework:

- What is your general impression of what this sonnet is about?
- Who is speaking? To whom?
- Is there a dominant image, or a variety of imagery?
- Which words, phrases or lines appeal to you the most?
- What is the sonnet's tone or mood?
- Is there a 'turn' (where the mood or meaning changes)?
- Which words or lines do you find difficult?
- Read the guidance provided on each sonnet page, then attempt the activity suggested.

After your preliminary discussion, choose one or more of the following activities:

a Prepare one or two questions about the sonnet to put to the whole class or to the teacher. The questions may concern features of the sonnet on which the group disagrees, or about which you feel puzzled.

b Make a short list of points which the group feels would help other students to understand and appreciate the sonnet.

c Suggest an appropriate title for the sonnet. Compare your title with other groups' titles.

d Prepare a set of notes to help someone who is about to give a public reading of the sonnet.

e Work out a shared reading of the sonnet. Use different voices for the different sections, and explore whether some lines could be spoken by more than one voice.

f Tape-record a reading of the sonnet. Experiment with sound effects, repetitions, echoes, length of pauses, and so on.

g Work out a dramatic presentation, such as a mime, to accompany and illustrate a reading of the sonnet.

2 Enlarging discussion

When the sonnet has been read aloud several times, work individually for five or ten minutes and write your own response to it. Afterwards, work in pairs, sharing and talking together about what you have written. Finally, move into groups of four, and after sharing views, each group makes a short report to the whole class.

3 A class debate

Divide the class into two groups. One side argues that the sonnet is part of Shakespeare's autobiography. The other side argues that it does not describe a real life experience, but is simply a literary exercise. The debate is likely to concern whether or not the sonnet seems sincere; whether or not you think that it expresses personal emotions in response to an actual event in Shakespeare's life (see pages 3–4).

4 Different interpretations

Take roles in the group, for example as a feminist critic, a psychoanalyst, a 'poetry hater', an actor, an examiner, William Shakespeare, a historian, a politician (name your party), the dark lady, and so on. Spend five or ten minutes thinking about what 'your' character's approach to the sonnet might be. Then engage in a whole-group discussion in which your task is to persuade other group members of the validity of 'your' view of the sonnet.

5 Illustrate a sonnet

Copy out and illustrate a sonnet. You may want to construct a collage of pictures from newspapers or magazines. Or, find a copy of William Blake's *Songs of Innocence and Experience*, and use that as your starting point.

6 Write your own sonnet

Imitation and parody are good ways in which to learn about structure, rhyme and rhythm. Follow Shakespeare's structure (you will find help on pages 1–2), but substitute words of your own. For example:

> Shall I compare thee to a … … ?
> Thou art more … and more … .

7 Reconstructing a sonnet

One person in each group copies out a chosen sonnet and then cuts it into fourteen strips. Each strip contains one line of the sonnet. Each group assembles their fourteen strips into a sequence. When all the groups have finished, compare your group's sequence with that of another group and also with Shakespeare's original sonnet, justifying your chosen order.

8 Shakespeare's other sonnets?

All Shakespeare's sonnets are about love. There are no sonnets which reveal his thoughts about the audiences at the Globe, about playing before the king, or about the pleasures and difficulties of play-writing. There is nothing about his fellow actors, or his own acting roles. He left no sonnets about his return visits to Stratford, his fellow townspeople, his family (he seems to have greatly disliked one of his sons-in-law, Thomas Quiney), or about why he left his second-best bed to his wife, Anne Hathaway.

Step into Shakespeare's shoes and write a sonnet about something other than love! You may find it helpful to start by using an existing sonnet as a framework.

9 Composite sonnets

It can be fascinating to use lines from different sonnets to assemble a new sonnet which Shakespeare never intended. Try your hand at making up such a sonnet, then list the benefits and losses of this kind of activity.

10 Points of view

All the sonnets are written from Shakespeare's point of view. They give one man's thoughts and feelings about the three other people in his life. What do you think would be the point of view of the young man, the dark lady, or the rival poet? Write a sonnet as one of these three, describing their feelings about Shakespeare.

11 Short list

You may only have a very limited time available for your work on *The Sonnets*. Every sonnet is rich in opportunities for discussion and appreciation, but if you feel you need help with selecting sonnets, the following are recommended: Sonnets 15, 16, 18, 29, 55, 73, 94, 116, 129, 130 and 144. They are usually judged to be among Shakespeare's finest, and they illustrate the major themes of the sequence. But don't hesitate to make your own selection!

12 Learning by heart

Learn a favoured sonnet by heart. Speak it at a class 'sonnet festival'.

Index of first lines

I grant thou wert not married to my Muse 82
I never saw that you did painting need 83
If my dear love were but the child of state 124
If the dull substance of my flesh were thought 44
If there be nothing new, but that which is 59
If thou survive my well-contented day 32
If thy soul check thee that I come so near 136
In faith, I do not love thee with mine eyes 141
In loving thee thou know'st I am forsworn 152
In the old age black was not counted fair 127
Is it for fear to wet a widow's eye 9
Is it thy will thy image should keep open 61

Let me confess that we two must be twain 36
Let me not to the marriage of true minds 116
Let not my love be called idolatry 105
Let those who are in favour with their stars 25
Like as the waves make towards the pebbled shore 60
Like as to make our appetites more keen 118
Lo, as a careful huswife runs to catch 143
Lo in the orient when the gracious light 7
Look in thy glass and tell the face thou viewest 3
Lord of my love, to whom in vassalage 26
Love is my sin, and thy dear virtue hate 142
Love is too young to know what conscience is 151

Mine eye and heart are at a mortal war 46
Mine eye hath played the painter and hath stelled 24
Music to hear, why hear'st thou music sadly? 8
My glass shall not persuade me I am old 22
My love is as a fever, longing still 147
My love is strength'ned, though more weak in seeming 102
My mistress' eyes are nothing like the sun 130
My tongue-tied Muse in manners holds her still 85

No longer mourn for me when I am dead 71
No more be grieved at that which thou hast done 35
No! Time, thou shalt not boast that I do change 123
Not from the stars do I my judgement pluck 14
Not marble nor the gilded monuments 55
Not mine own fears, nor the prophetic soul 107

O call not me to justify the wrong 139
O for my sake do you with Fortune chide 111
O from what pow'r hast thou this pow'rful might 150

Those lines that I before have writ do lie   115
Those lips that Love's own hand did make   145
Those parts of thee that the world's eye doth view   69
Those pretty wrongs that liberty commits   41
Thou art as tyrannous, so as thou art   131
Thou blind fool, Love, what dost thou to mine eyes   137
Thus can my love excuse the slow offence   51
Thus is his cheek the map of days outworn   68
Thy bosom is endearèd with all hearts   31
Thy gift, thy tables, are within my brain   122
Thy glass will show thee how thy beauties wear   77
Tired with all these, for restful death I cry   66
'Tis better to be vile than vile esteemed   121
To me, fair friend, you never can be old   104
Two loves I have, of comfort and despair   144

Unthrifty loveliness, why dost thou spend   4

Was it the proud full sail of his great verse   86
Weary with toil, I haste me to my bed   27
Were't aught to me I bore the canopy   125
What is your substance, whereof are you made   53
What potions have I drunk of Siren tears   119
What's in the brain that ink may character   108
When forty winters shall besiege thy brow   2
When I consider every thing that grows   15
When I do count the clock that tells the time   12
When I have seen by Time's fell hand defaced   64
When in disgrace with Fortune and men's eyes   29
When in the chronicle of wasted time   106
When most I wink, then do mine eyes best see   43
When my love swears that she is made of truth   138
When thou shalt be disposed to set me light   88
When to the sessions of sweet silent thought   30
Where art thou, Muse, that thou forget'st so long   100
Whilst I alone did call upon thy aid   79
Who is it that says most which can say more   84
Who will believe my verse in time to come   17
Whoever hath her wish, thou hast thy Will   135
Why didst thou promise such a beauteous day   34
Why is my verse so barren of new pride?   76

Your love and pity doth th'impression fill   112

William Shakespeare 1564–1616

1564 Born Stratford-upon-Avon, eldest son of John and Mary Shakespeare.
1582 Marries Anne Hathaway of Shottery, near Stratford.
1583 Daughter, Susanna, born.
1585 Twins, son and daughter, Hamnet and Judith, born.
1592 First mention of Shakespeare in London. Robert Greene, another play wright, describes Shakespeare as 'an upstart crow beautified with our feathers…'. Greene seems to have been jealous of Shakespeare. He mocked Shakespeare's name, calling him 'the only Shake-scene in a country' (presumably because Shakespeare was writing successful plays).
1595 A shareholder in 'The Lord Chamberlain's Men', an acting company that becomes extremely popular.
1596 Son Hamnet dies, aged eleven.
Father, John, granted arms (acknowledged as a gentleman).
1597 Buys New Place, the grandest house in Stratford.
1598 Acts in Ben Jonson's *Every Man in His Humour*.
1599 Globe Theatre opens on Bankside. Performances in the open air.
1601 Father, John, dies.
1603 James I grants Shakespeare's company a royal patent: 'The Lord Chamberlain's Men' become 'The King's Men' and play about twelve performances each year at court.
1607 Daughter, Susanna, marries Dr John Hall.
1608 Mother, Mary, dies.
1609 'The King's Men' begin performing indoors at Blackfriars Theatre.
1610 Probably returns from London to live in Stratford.
1616 Daughter, Judith, marries Thomas Quiney.
Dies. Buried in Holy Trinity Church, Stratford-upon-Avon.

The plays and poems
(no one knows exactly when he wrote each play)

1589–1595 *The Two Gentlemen of Verona, The Taming of the Shrew, First, Second and Third Parts of King Henry VI, Titus Andronicus, King Richard III, The Comedy of Errors, Love's Labour's Lost, A Midsummer Night's Dream, Romeo and Juliet, King Richard II* (and the long poems *Venus and Adonis* and *The Rape of Lucrece*).
1596–1599 *King John, The Merchant of Venice, First and Second Parts of King Henry IV, The Merry Wives of Windsor, Much Ado About Nothing, King Henry V, Julius Caesar* (and probably *The Sonnets*).
1600–1605 *As You Like It, Hamlet, Twelfth Night, Troilus and Cressida, Measure for Measure, Othello, All's Well That Ends Well, Timon of Athens, King Lear.*
1606–1611 *Macbeth, Antony and Cleopatra, Pericles, Coriolanus, The Winter's Tale, Cymbeline, The Tempest.*
1613 *King Henry VIII, The Two Noble Kinsmen* (both probably with John Fletcher).
1623 Shakespeare's plays published as a collection (now called the First Folio).